PORTSMOUTH POINT

PORTSMOUTH POINT, by Thomas Rowlandson, *circa* 1799

PORTSMOUTH POINT

The Navy in Fiction

1793 - 1815

•

C. NORTHCOTE PARKINSON

LIVERPOOL
UNIVERSITY PRESS

First published 1949 by
Liverpool University Press
4 Cambridge Street
Liverpool L69 7ZU

This edition published 2005

British Library Cataloguing-in-Publication data
A British Library CIP record is available

SBN 0-85323-139-7

Typeset by Koinonia, Bury
Printed and bound in the European Union
by Bell and Bain Ltd, Glasgow

FOR JILL

CONTENTS

LIST OF ILLUSTRATIONS

PREFACE

It is at Portsmouth Point that the reader is invited to take his stand. The year is 1799, and we know—for Rowlandson has drawn the scene for us—what we shall notice as we pause to stare. There is the slop-dealer, there the tavern. We can all but hear the noise and confusion as barrels roll and women scream or fight. The gulls are crying, the boats are plying from the shore, and, beyond all, at anchor, lie the King's ships of that day. Here is a boat for hire and there is a frigate we may go aboard. Shall we venture, or has the reader seen enough?

Viewing the Point through Rowlandson's eyes, we see, and clearly, all there is to see. But here at Portsmouth he is, in truth, almost as lost as we ourselves. He is but a stranger from London on his first and only visit. If we are to visit the ships and talk with those we find on board, we shall need guides who understand. And here they are: Captain Marryat, whom we have often met before; Captain Chamier whom we know at least by name; some gentlemen whose acquaintance we are glad to make; and a few whose names we somehow fail to catch.

Are these guides sufficient? There are those who will deny it. Here, they will object, are mere writers of fiction. Sailors they may be but born, it seems, too late; too late to have served with Nelson, too late to be with us in 1799. Why, they will protest, should we not prefer to rely upon actual memoirs, dating, beyond question, from the period named? It would be absurd to make much parade of scholarship in a book planned mainly for entertainment. This much, however, must be said in its defence: there is that to be learnt from fiction which can be learnt in no other way; we can use only the fiction that exists; and we should be foolish to mingle it with fact.

A good novel is true to its period in atmosphere. The characters are imaginary, the events never took place, but the setting is real. More than that, the novelist, in writing his dialogue, has not to tax his memory for the exact words used. He writes boldly the sort of talk there might have been and so creates—as compared with the biographer—an impression more vivid and, in a sense, more true. William James, the naval historian, tells us much about the French Wars in the six volumes of his History, but it is only the readers of Marryat who can visualise the events he is trying to describe. Had we, in fact, to choose between them, we might think Marryat the better historian of the two.

Fiction, then, has its place. As regards the passages quoted, however, the choice has been haphazard enough. Many works of merit will, no doubt, have been overlooked. Nor may the anthologist assume that the reader's assessment of value will coincide with his. Of the novels quoted those by Marryat are unquestionably the best. Only a·limited use has been made of them, however, as the books themselves are easy to obtain. To those the reader is referred. On the same principle are excluded those few admirable pages in which Jane Austen shows, tantalisingly, her knowledge of the naval officer as seen ashore. Use has been made, for preference, of works less popular than hers; books more or less forgotten by authors more or less obscure.

The books used date, with one or two exceptions, from the period from 1826 to 1848, while relating to the war years which ended in 1815. All the authors had first-hand knowledge of the Navy. Some, like Davis, Marryat, Glascock, Barker, Howard, and Hall are known to have been at sea before 1815, though mostly not before 1805. Others, like Neale and Hannay, went to sea only after the war was over. Most of the fiction quoted can be regarded, then, as direct evidence of naval life in, say, 1810-15. But for Nelson's time, properly considered, the evidence is hearsay. That is not to say that it is valueless. There were changes in the Service after 1805 but there was much also that did not change. And if the authors had not gone to sea in 1793 they had served with many men who had.

It would be more satisfactory, nevertheless, if more than two of the novels quoted bore a published date earlier than 1826. That more do not is scarcely the anthologist's fault, however, for the novel in the modern sense—and especially the novel of historical value—practically begins with Jane Austen. Earlier novels cannot be quoted because they were not written. This fact is strikingly illustrated in what is almost the earliest work quoted, *The Post Captain*, published in 1805. For, whereas parts of that book—and notably the passages quoted—are invaluable, the rest of the story is in the Smollett tradition, improbable, broadly caricatured, and little to our purpose.

While firmly insisting upon the value of this nearly contemporary fiction, especially in the absence of anything written earlier, one is surely justified, on the other hand, in refusing to mingle it with fact. The truth enshrined in *Midshipman Easy* or *Tom Bowling* is not of the same order as that found in, say, a *Memoir of the Life of Admiral Sir Edward Codrington*, by his daughter. To have Lord Nelson and Peter Simple on the same plane, on the same quarter-deck, would embarrass all concerned, and the reader most of all. Wise is the Captain Hornblower who avoids all but the most distant acquaintance with his more historical contemporaries. That the events and persons in fiction have their basis in fact is not to be disputed, but they are bound—like Mr." Walt Disney's cartoon characters—by their own conventions. The precedent of *Ben Brace* is hardly one to follow.

The authors quoted have, many of them, a tendency to dwell gloomily on the brutalities and discomforts of life afloat. It is a tendency less observable in the writers of avowed reminiscence. Some of this gloom may originate with Smollett. More may be due to a reaction following the hero-worship of Southey's *Nelson*, published in 1813. Most of all, perhaps, may arise from the authors having served in the later years of a war no longer epic but just drearily prolonged. But when all this is admitted, it is only fair to add that there was a degree of pessimism inherent in the naval character long before their time. It is implicit, for one thing, in many of Charles Dibdin's songs, which were popular among the sailors themselves. There is an authentic professional cynicism in lines like these:—

> *Then to see the tight lads, how they laugh at a stranger*
> *Who fears billows can drown, and nine-pounders can kill!*
> *For you're safe, sure enough, were you not in such danger,*
> *And might loll at your ease, if you could but sit still.*
> *What of perils that, always the same, are so various,*
> *And though shot-holes and leaks leave wide open Death's door?*
> *Devil a risk's in a battle, were't not so precarious;*
> *Storms were all gig and fun, but for breakers and shores.*
> *In short, a tar's life—you may say that I told it—*
> *Who leaves quiet and peace, foreign countries to roam,*
> *Is, of all other lives, I'll be bound to uphold it,*
> *The best life in the world, next to staying at home.*

With these verses we are fairly back at the Point and ready to embark, accepting what guidance is offered us, and ready, it is hoped, to make allowance for the shortcomings in our entertainment. As we peer again at Rowlandson's drawing, perhaps we can see the figures move and grow larger at our approach. Dodging the pugnacious lady on the left—did you hear her language?—and pausing to tip the one-legged fiddler, we are now at the quay. Here is our wherry and there, over the water, is the *Apollo* frigate of 38 guns. Much of the rest the reader must picture for himself.

> *Play with your fancies, and in them behold*
> *Upon the hempen tackle ship-boys climbing;*
>   *Hear the shrill whistle which doth order give*
> *To sounds confused . . .*
>   *. . . o do but think*
> *You stand upon the rivage, and behold*
> *A City on the inconstant billows dancing;*
>   *For so appears this fleet majestical. . . .*

C. NORTHCOTE PARKINSON.

University of Liverpool,
   January, 1948.

CHAPTER I

THE MAN-OF-WAR

Ships of the line have their place in history books, frigates theirs in fiction. Most of the material here quoted relates to frigates and the accompanying illustrations are intended to give some idea of what a frigate looked like. At the beginning of the French Wars in 1793 the frigates available numbered only 61, as compared with 113 sail of the line, and 75 sixth-rates and sloops. As the war progressed, more ships were needed for commerce protection but ships of the line did not multiply to the same extent. There were, indeed, only 108 of them in commission in 1810: by which year the cruisers (frigates, sloops, brigs, and cutters) numbered no less than 664. The frigates then in commission numbered 133. They fell, roughly, into three classes: 38-gun frigates, of which there were 48; 36-gun frigates, of which there were 49; and 32-gun frigates, of which there were 31.

A typical ship of the large class was the "Diana," built to the design of Sir J. Henslow in 1794. She measured 146 feet 3 inches on the gun-deck, and 998 tons. She was established for a crew of 274. She mounted twenty-eight 18-pounders, with eight 9-pounders on the quarter-deck and two on the forecastle. Her sister ship, the "Jason," built in the same year, mounted four 32-pounder carronades on her quarter-deck instead of the long guns and two more on her forecastle. Carronades were then popular and by 1799 all frigates had them.

The extract given below relates to the "Apollo." A long succession of frigates bore that name from 1794 onwards. But the author, in describing "The between decks of the 'Apollo,'" adds that his description will serve as well "for all the frigates that ever were built, or ever will."

This deck then was just five feet five inches high to the beams, or cross timbers, by some thirty-six or forty feet wide from side to side, and required a sort of reverential position when walking, as a man even of the sailor breed, or under middle size, was sure to knock his pate against this ribbed ceiling. Thus, on descending into these regions of darkness, the hat was pulled off with great expedition, and the traveller advanced in the same position ambassadors advance towards thrones: it has been supposed, we will not say with how much justice, that this continual lowly position causes the round-shouldered stoop observable in the sons of Neptune; be this as it may, the whole expanse as far as visible forward, through the misty darkness, presented nothing but a succession of these ribs overhead. Those next the mainmast (opposite to which was situate the berth, parlour, or drawing-room of the mids) might be seen thick-studded with the hats and belts of the marines in all stages of pipe-claying, polishing, and brushing, together with their other accoutrements, *dangling in mid air* from their batons, while the soldiers themselves filled up the space beneath, busy as bees in the said operation; two exact rows of hanging tables garnished either side; and the rest of more irregular jacks filled up a confused distance into the very bows. Opposite the table of the marines lay a gulf called the main hatchway—this yawned terrible, displaying huge cables coiled in their tiers, and winding upwards to daylight held (running along the main deck above) this floating castle at her anchors; in the middle, amidships, just before the spot, stood, filing and hammering, two grim personages who might have passed for a pair of the cyclops, amidst the din, to which their noise came in, as the drum in a full band, the other instruments being a mixture of mouths in full chorus; the pipes of the boatswain's mate, the shrill squeaking of the *ladies*, with other sounds too confused to particularise.

Immediately behind all this, and on the opposite side, balancing the *parlour* of the midshipmen, lay constructed exactly in the same manner, the cabin of the captain's steward—a person of infinite consequence—where many good things were discussed besides politics, viz., at least one-half of his master's eatables and drinkables. . . .

Behind this temple, on the same side, lived two quiet creatures, of little note in the neighbourhood, and considered a couple of old bores by the whole set of bloods, whose chests and toilets came in contact with the outside of their partition. These poor souls were no other than the *gunner* and *carpenter* of the ship—warrant officers and men of note and authority on deck, but wholly insignificant at home . . . they never gained ground, or received any advance on the score of intimacy with the bucks of the quarter-deck, on the larboard side, except the good natured scribe Toby, considered an amphibious animal whose bureau, or office, lay exactly opposite, and separated only from the mids by the cabin of the boatswain. . . .   [See plate 3, page 45].

We have now comprehended the whole area of the steerage—of that space included between the hallowed partition, or *bulkhead*, which separated the awful cabins of the lieutenants, and the foremost verge of the mids' and captain's stewards' cabins on each side, between which

PLATE 1—Early 19th Century Captain's Uniform.

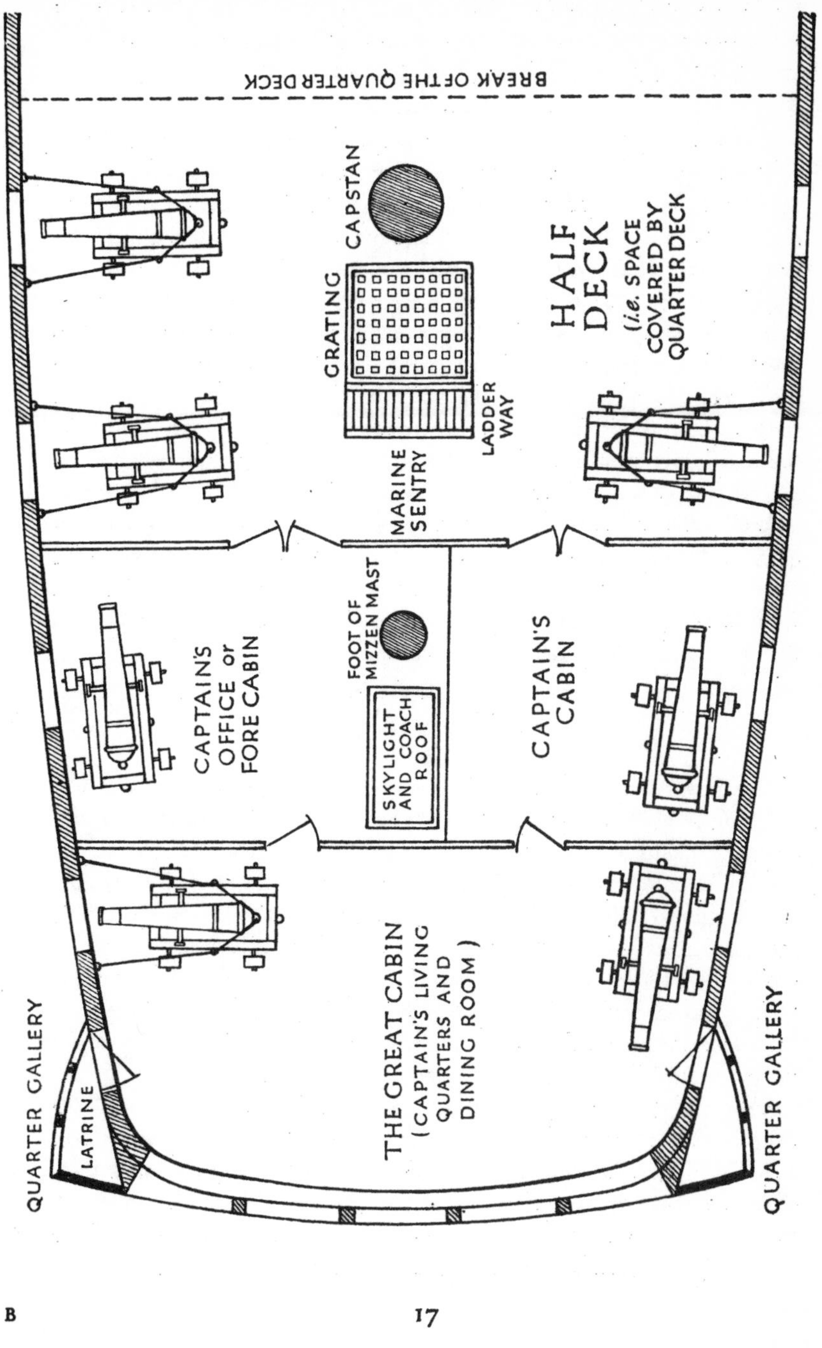

BREAK OF THE QUARTER DECK

CAPSTAN

GRATING

HALF DECK
(*i.e.* SPACE COVERED BY QUARTER DECK)

MARINE SENTRY

LADDER WAY

CAPTAIN'S OFFICE or FORE CABIN

FOOT OF MIZZEN MAST

SKYLIGHT AND COACH ROOF

CAPTAIN'S CABIN

THE GREAT CABIN
(CAPTAIN'S LIVING QUARTERS AND DINING ROOM)

QUARTER GALLERY

LATRINE

QUARTER GALLERY

PLATE 2.—Great Cabin, coach and half-deck of a 38-gun frigate.

B

17

came down in mighty volume, the mainmast, and all the pumps, great shores or stanchions, etc., forming a sort of thick wood or forest—the scene of many skirmishes between the belligerents in night attacks.

The Navy at Home (3 Vols., London, 1831. William Marsh).

————•◆•————

I turned, on descending the hatchway, to view the maindeck. Ye gods, what a difference ! I had anticipated a kind of elegant house with guns in the windows; an orderly set of men; in short, I expected to find a species of Grosvenor Place floating about like Noah's ark. Here were the tars of England rolling about casks, without jackets, shoes, or stockings. On one side provisions were received on board; at one port-hole coals, at another wood; dirty women, the objects of sailors' affections, with beer cans in hand, were everywhere conspicuous; the shrill whistle squeaked, and the voice of the boatswain and his mates rattled like thunder in my ears; the deck was dirty, slippery, and wet; the smells abominable; the whole sight disgusting; and when I remarked the slovenly dress of the midshipmen, dressed in shabby round jackets, glazed hats, no gloves, and some without shoes, I forgot all the glory of Nelson, all the pride of the navy, the terror of France, or the bulwark of Albion; and for nearly the first time in my life, and I wish I could say it was the last, took the handkerchief from my pocket, covered my face, and cried like the child I was.

The Life of a Sailor. By a captain in the Navy (3 vols., London, 1832. Richard Bentley).

————•◆•————

The next moment he stood in the presence of the captain, who was reclining on a sofa in the after-cabin, where was blended a strange medley of rough tokens of war with the softer attributes of peace; here ranged, well-filled book cases—there, double-barreled pistols, and Turkish and French sabres. Here polished mahogany satin chairs, vases of flowers, and billet-doux—there, stern cold iron in the shape of eighteen pounders, taking their way through windows (the ports) hung with silk curtains— their icy touch and strained lashings told their scorn of the painter's art to render them less ferocious, in white and green—in the fore-cabin hung a beautiful ormolu lamp over a festive board, where, when at sea, smoked eight silver covers at least (every day at 4 p.m.), with all the delicacies of all the world—now garnished with a fine green cloth, cut-glass decanters, different sorts of wine, and a luncheon on a tray, after the most approved modes of the fashionable world. In short, all was of the most refined elegance, of the most approved taste, of the most exquisite delicacy, and of the richest description, side by side, with the instruments of stern and instant destruction. In five minutes all would disappear, and the dogs let slip, fire, smoke, cartridges, bleeding bodies, recoiled guns; and fifty devils incarnate would turn this floating paradise to a hellish pandemoniun !

The Navy at Home. (3 Vols. London, 1831. William Marsh.)

I was stationed at the foremast guns on the maindeck, and the ship cleared for action; and though on a comparatively small scale, I cannot imagine a more solemn, grand, or impressive sight than a ship prepared as ours was on that occasion. Her noble tier of guns in a line gently curving out towards the centre: the tackle laid across the deck; the shots and wads prepared in ample store (round shot and canister); the powder boys each with his box full, seated on it, with perfect apparent indifference as to the approaching conflict. The captains of guns, with their priming boxes buckled round their waists; the locks fixed upon the guns; the lanyards laid around them; the officers, with their swords drawn, standing by their respective divisions.

The quarter-deck was commanded by the captain in person, assisted by the first lieutenant, the lieutenant of marines, a party of small-arm men, with the mate and midshipmen, and a portion of seamen to attend the braces and fight the quarter-deck guns. The boatswain was on the forecastle; the gunner in the magazine to send up a supply of powder to the guns; the carpenter watched and reported, from time to time, the depth of water in the well. He was attended by his mates, who were provided with shot-plugs, oakum, and tallow, to stop any shot holes which might be made.

The surgeon was in the cockpit with his assistants. The knives, saws, tourniquets, sponges, basins, wine and water, were all displayed and ready for the first unlucky patient that might be presented. This was more awful to me than anything I had seen. . . .

As soon as the fleet bore up to engage the enemy, we did the same, keeping as near as we could to the admiral, whose signals we were ordered to repeat. I was particularly astonished with the skilful manner in which this was done. It was wonderful to see how instantaneously the same flags were displayed at our mastheads as had been hoisted by the admiral; and the more wonderful this appeared to me, since his flags were rolled up in round balls, which were not broke loose until they had reached the masthead, so that the signal officers of a repeater had to make out the number of the flag during its passage aloft in disguise. This was done by the power of good telescopes, and from habit, and sometimes by anticipation of the signal that would be next made.

The reader may perhaps not be aware that among civilized nations, in naval warfare, ships in the line never fire at frigates, unless they provoke hostility by interposing between belligerent ships, or firing into them, as was the case in the Nile, when Sir James Saumarez, in the *Orion*, was under the necessity of sinking the *Artemise*, which he did with one broadside, as a reward for her temerity. Under this *pax-in-bellum* sort of compact, we might have come off scot-free, had we not partaken very liberally of the shot intended for larger ships, which did us serious damage.

Frank Mildmay, or The Naval Officer. Capt. Marryat (London, 1829).

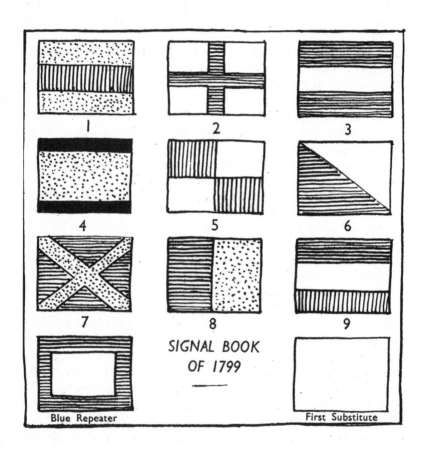

SIGNAL BOOK
OF 1799

CHAPTER II

THE OFFICERS

A man-of-war might be commanded either by a post captain, a "master and commander," or a lieutenant. Any ship with more than twenty-eight guns would normally be commanded by an officer of post-rank. A sloop, whether a ship or a brig, might have either a captain or a "master and commander." A schooner or cutter was usually under the command of a lieutenant. The title of "master and commander" was used only in official correspondence, an officer of that rank being addressed, particularly by his subordinates and by his friends ashore, as "captain." A lieutenant in charge of a cutter was never called "captain" save in deliberate flattery. Like other lieutenants, his proper title was his surname, prefixed by the word "Mister."

The achieving of post-rank was, in a sense, the climax of a naval officer's career. It was the highest rank to which either interest or exertion could raise him. Thenceforward, provided he were employed, his promotion was a matter of seniority and could scarcely be hastened by any efforts of his own. To become an admiral, the essential steps were to be made post early and then to outlive the officers immediately senior. A tough constitution was the first requisite for success. Everything, however, depended on a rapid attainment of the rank of captain. Officers with very great interest, especially the sons of admirals, were often posted at a very early age. Captains aged nineteen or twenty were not unknown. There were cases of boys being promoted at as early an age as seventeen, and an older generation had seen at least one captain who had not yet reached that age.

The distinction drawn in later Stuart times between "gentlemen" and "tarpaulin" commanders never entirely disappeared during the 18th century. The profession was still open to talent and many officers had little or no pretension to gentility. There was, however, growing up a secondary or professional idea of rank. Officers of a normal middle-class origin frequently managed to acquire the accent and manners of the gentry without learning to despise their own trade; and it was among these that many of the best commanders were to be found. The Captain Wentworth portrayed by Jane Austen was a man of comparatively humble origin but perfectly able to move in the polite society of Bath. His good manners did not prevent him, nevertheless, from being perfectly frank about his pursuit of *"prize-money."* He was making his fortune in a business-like way and saw no reason to be ashamed of it. *Alongside officers of this admirable type were to be found the younger sons of the gentry and nobility. Some of these, by conceit and affectation, drove their messmates to the other extreme, so that there were captains who made rather a boast of their plebian birth and a virtue of their ill manners. A bluff "sea-dog" air was often a sort of protest against foppery, and did not even indicate a particularly lowly origin.*

A captain, then, might be of almost any age, from twenty to fifty, and of almost any social rank. After 1815 the reduction of the Navy gave scope to a wave of snobbishness which brought about the ultimate exclusion of the plebeian officer.

The sun had just streaked the eastern hemisphere with his rays, when the commander of a frigate, which was cruising in the British Channel, awoke; and giving a monstrous yawn, called to a sentry at the cabin-door to pass the word for the steward. The sentry was walking to and fro under the half-deck, armed with a huge cutlass, which for more than a year had not slept in a scabbard; and, on hearing the order, he applied his hands to his mouth, vociferating with the lungs of a stentor, "Pass the word there for the captain's steward!"

Our Captain next took a miniature from under his pillow, which he seemed to contemplate with peculiar delight; sighing and soliloquizing as he hung over it enamoured: "Can any face," cried he, "be more angelic? Such top-lights! Or can any form be more ravishing? Such a pair of cat-heads! And, oh! what hair! By ——, one might take a sheep-shank in it! Blow my good breeze! Fill all my sails! driver and ring-tail, spritsail and sprit-topsail! flying jib and jib of jibs! Waft me, oh waft me to the arms of Cassandra!"

The Post-Captain, or The Wooden Walls well manned; comprehending a view of naval society and manners. John Davis. (First published in 1805. Thomas Tegg. Reprinted, 1928).

———————•———————

The joke about the seaman's vocabulary when in love was no novelty in 1805. It had been one of the standing jests of the eighteenth century and was as familiar to Congreve as to Smollett. In putting this soliloquy into his captain's mouth, Davis was following tradition. There was, nevertheless, a basis for the satire, even at a later period of the nineteenth century. The language of the sailor often remained distinctive, if only to answer to popular expectation. He was encouraged to be unintelligible exactly as Scotsmen have been so encouraged.

22

The school of naval captains most remarkable is one which may be called the "Benbow school," from its adherence to the old customs of the service. The captain of this school thinks that the service is going to the devil. He uses a speaking trumpet, and wears a broad-tailed coat. He looks with abhorrence upon a man who can reason, or speak fluently, and calls him a "sea lawyer." He impresses upon the minds of his officers that they have no right to think, and sets an example by never thinking himself. . . . He has divine service performed every Sunday, and regularly goes to sleep during the sermon. He "wonders what the navy will come to," when he sees claret in a midshipman's mess. He discourages taking in journals and goes to sleep after dinner. He flogs the men often "on system," and pronounces a youngster, who shows any affectionate remembrance of home, a milksop. He always holds the same political opinions as the ministry that is in; and is very much afraid of the admiral. . . .

The opposite class to this, is the class of dashing dandy captains, who have pianofortes in their cabins—give parties on board—go out partridge shooting—and find their duty a bore. These gentlemen cultivate the acquaintance of the military, and are proud of losing their money at blind-hookey. In fact, they try to turn the vessels they command into yachts, and succeed in degrading them from the rank of men-of-war, but not in obtaining any elegance to make up for the loss of their utility. . . . .

Biscuits and Grog. The personal reminiscences and sketches of Percival Plug, R.N. (Late Midshipman of H.M.S. *Preposterous.*) Second edition. James Hannay. London, 1848. John and D. A. Darling.

———————•———————

The above extract dates, as will be seen, from a late period. It is to be observed, however, that reminiscences of this kind usually relate to a time somewhat before the date of publication. The "Benbow school" of captains, moreover, was actually a relic of the Nelson period. The officers described belonged to an earlier age, and it is of no great consequence that Hannay can have seen them only in rather later life. If they then spent much of their time in bewailing the decadence of the service, it is at least clear that there was, in fact, a great deal of decadence to bewail.

The following quotation illustrates the gulf which divided the commander of a frigate from the commander of a cutter. The officers and midshipmen who served in such small craft were always looked down upon as creatures very low in the social scale. Between the post captain of a frigate and the "master and commander" of a sloop there was a gulf, but not of quite the same kind. Every rising man had to be a "master and commander" at some time or other of his career. To command a cutter in the

Channel, on the other hand, was not a necessary step to further promotion. Such a vessel was commanded, as often as not, by an elderly ex-boatswain, promoted to lieutenant for the purpose and almost certain to retire with that rank.

Oddly enough, while the captain of a frigate despised those below him in the hierarchy, he was often very much inclined to pity those immediately above him. The captain of a ship of the line had comparatively little chance either of making prize-money or distinguishing himself. The novelist's hero always commanded a frigate.

Towards noon, a cutter appeared in sight; signals by telegraph quickly gave our Captain to understand that there were both news and despatches. The sea had by this time gone down considerably, which enabled a bandy-legged officer, dressed in tights and Hessian boots, with a tarnished cocked hat, which came up first, and a shabby epaulette, which quickly followed, to mount the gangway. This specimen of naval architecture (his shoulders were as round as a barrel) placed a sealed packet in the Captain's hands, who had no sooner perused it than he made a very slight bow to the bearer, then touching his hat at the same time, with an expression of countenance which plainly signified "get out," he ordered the boatswain to turn the hands up —— make sail!

The officer in the tights thought this was sharp practice, so was down the side in an instant, and ordered his-boat's crew to pull back to his own craft. He knew he was a lion in the cutter—worse than a mouse in the huge fabric he had joyously quitted—he gained his own quarter-deck, snapped his fingers at his big friend to windward, and then ordered his boatswain (mate) to pipe to grog—his allowance was no joke, as he kept the key.

The Indiaman. By a Blue Jacket. Vol. II. (London, 1840. Richard Bentley.

————•————

Next in importance to the Captain was the First Lieutenant. The nature of this office varied considerably with the character of the Captain. In ships commanded by mere boys, promoted by interest, the first lieutenant was usually an old and steady officer and often the real ruler of the ship. Such a man was said to be acting as "dry-nurse" to his nominal superior. The faithful performance of this thankless task seems rarely to have earned promotion. Not infrequently an officer's usefulness as "dry-nurse" was made a reason for not advancing him. In much the same way, an old captain, worn out by long service and only waiting for his flag—that is, for promotion to the rank of Rear-Admiral—before retiring, often came to leave the entire management of his ship to his second-in-command. An able and active captain, on the other hand, would leave his first lieutenant with no more than his proper responsibility.

There was a strong tendency for some seamen to remain fixed as lieutenants for half a lifetime. An experienced but uncouth officer often failed to rise any higher. There were, therefore, in the service, a great number of elderly first lieutenants, who did most of the work and received but little of the credit for it. If without interest, their only hope of promotion lay in their chance of distinguishing themselves in action; and for many of them this chance never came. A lieutenant aged fifty, with nothing to look forward to but the meagre half-pay of his rank, was often an embittered man, the terror of his subordinates. An officer of this type, who had usually started life in a merchant ship or before the mast, was sometimes as careless in dress as he was caustic in speech.

Being safely landed on the quarter-deck of the frigate, I literally shrunk back through a feeling of intense admiration, approaching to awe, at the scene which presented itself: where nautical neatness, accurate arrangement, intricate machinery, and moving masses of men completed the illusion, and overwhelmed the mind with the gigantic grandeur of the whole.

As I cautiously stepped on the deck, my eyes attracted by the alternate whiteness of the planks and polished ebony of the parallel caulking, my ears were assailed by sounds which seemed to threaten danger aloft, proceeding from the thunder-like claps of the shivering sails, as they hung in the brails, and flapped their huge wings in the wind.

In this state of apprehension from undefined danger, and motionless as a statue, I felt myself pulled by the sleeve. The Black had been enjoying my surprise, and now motioned me to make my obeisance to a vulgar-looking, squat, round-shouldered man, whose obliquity of vision exposed every being he looked at to a sort of cross fire, from eyes which appeared to have a roving commission. A "voice like a boatswain" had been a phrase with my father, and the association was revived by the stentor-like tones of this strange-looking person, who was dressed in a blue white-edged coat, which displayed here and there a few straggling anchor-buttons of different dies—to which was added a buff, soup-spotted vest, a pair of tarred nankeen trowsers, and an old battered broad-brimmed leathern hat. This homely habit, with divers distinguishable daubings of pitch or whitewash on his back, naturally induced me to conclude he could be no other than the Boatswain. I was soon undeceived. . . . [It was the First Lieutenant.]

The Naval Sketch-Book. By an Officer of Rank. (Second edition. London, 1826.) Henry Colburn.

"When I was quarter-master on board of the *Melpomene*, we had an old chap for first lieutenant whose name was Fletcher. He was a kind-hearted man enough, as he never worried the ship's company when there was no occasion; but at the same time, he was what you call a stickler for duty—made no allowances for neglect or disobedience of orders, although he could wink at any little sky-larking, walking aft, shutting his eyes, and pretending not to see or hear it. His usual phrase was: 'My man, you've got your duty to do, and I've got mine.' And this he repeated fifty times a day; so at last he went by the name of 'Old Duty.' I think I see him now, walking up and down with his spy-glass under his left arm, and the hand of the other pushed into his breast, as if he were fumbling for a flea. His hat was always split, and worn in the front from constantly taking it off instead of touching it, when he came on the quarter-deck; and as soon as it was too far gone in front to raise the purchase off his head, he used to shift it end for end, bringing the back part in front, and then he would wear it until, as the Yankees say, it was in 'taterations altogether'; and he was forced to bend a new one.

"Now we had a boy on board, who entered one day when the captain landed at Torquay to dine with a friend. His name was Jack Jervis and his father and his whole tribe had been fishermen for as long as could be remembered . . . and he was never so happy as when his line was overboard, or when he was snooding a hook in some corner or another. He went by the name of Jack the Fisherman, and a smart, active, willing lad he was, sure enough.

"Now there was a little difficulty between Old Duty and Jack the Fisherman. Old Duty would not allow the lines to be overboard when the ship was in harbour; as he said it was untidy in appearance, and there was always plenty of work and no time for fishing. So Jack hadn't pulled up his line ten or a dozen times before he was pulled up himself. "Whose line's that?" says Old Duty. "Mine, sir," says Jack, touching his hat. "I don't allow fishing, young man," said the first lieutenant. "You understand me? I don't allow fishing. You've your duty to do, sir, and I've got mine."

"Jack, who had been only two or three days on board, and who, I believe, would never have entered, had he known that there would have been such a '*weto*,' as the boatswain used to call it, looked quite astonished, and said:—

" 'What, mayn't I fish, sir!'

" 'No, my man, you must not fish without permission; and that I never give in harbour. If I catch you fishing again, you get two dozen at the gun; recollect that. You've got your duty to do, and I've got mine.'

"Well, Jack could not give up his habit, so he used to fish at night, and all night long, out of the fore-chains; but it so happened that the ship's corporal caught Jack in the middle watch, and reports him to the first lieutenant.

" 'So, you've been fishing again, sir,' says Old Duty. 'No, sir,' replied Jack, 'not fishing—only laying night lines.'

" 'Oh! that's it,' replied the first lieutenant; 'only laying night lines ! Pray, what's the difference?' 'Please, sir,' said Jack, touching his hat, 'the difference is——that it's not the same thing.'

"Well, sir, I see but one difference, and I'll meet it accordingly. You've your duty to do, and I've got mine.'

" 'The boys' heads and ears having been pulled about and examined by the master-at-arms, they were dismissed; and Jack thought that he had got off—but he was mistaken.

"After the hammocks had been piped down, and it was dark, the boys were ordered up by the master-at-arms; Jack was seized to the gun, and had his two dozen. 'There, sir,' said Old Duty, as they cast the seizings off, 'if fishing at night is not fishing, punishment at night is not punishment. Now, we're quits. You've your duty to do, and I've got mine.' "

Poor Jack. By Captain Marryat, C.B. (London, 1846. Longmans.)

————•————

A frigate had an establishment, in 1793, of three lieutenants; ships of the line five and upwards. In the following extract from the "Naval Sketch Book," the junior officers are given a rather higher social status than the senior; a state of affairs very typical of the period. It was often the case that a second or third lieutenant had far better prospects than his immediate senior. With the lieutenants messed the marine officer or officers, the master, the surgeon, and the purser. Marine officers had less to do than perhaps anyone else on board. In the literature of the period they are always represented as dividing their time between gluttony and sleep. As few of them could rise above the rank of captain, which was equal to lieutenant in the navy, and none above the rank of major, they were seldom men of either birth or talent. The master, whose principal function was as navigational expert, had almost invariably been in the merchant service. He was not a commissioned officer but, like the purser, he held his warrant from the Admiralty. Very occasionally, as a reward for distinguished service, a master would be made a lieutenant. As a rule, however, the only promotion he could look for was transference to a larger ship and ultimately, perhaps, a flagship. If he was very fortunate, he might end his days as master attendant at one of the dockyards. The purser had usually begun his career as a captain's clerk. He could seek preferment in a ship of a higher rate, and he might ultimately have a post on shore as storekeeper.

Dinner being at last announced by beat of drum, down flew the officers, helter-skelter, to the gun-room, the start being decidedly in favour of the lieutenant of marines, a light-infantry-like figure of about fifteen-stone weight. The surgeon, however, who appeared to be the most civilized civilian on board, struck with my forlorn situation, returned, and looking up the hatchway, beckoned me good-naturedly to follow him below. Encouraged by this kindness, I descended cautiously both the quarter and the main-deck ladders leading to the steerage, abaft which, in the gun-room, dinner was served up. Thither my guide and I groped our way in the dark, breaking our shins against the midshipmen's chests. . . . [The gun-room was] a dismal dungeon-like looking place, flanked on each side by a row of miserably cramped cribs, called cabins. Overhead there was certainly what, by some poetic licence, continued to be denominated a skylight; but, as to any light afforded, it might as well have been under foot, most of the panes in its frame having been fractured, and unpainted patches of solid wood substituted for what had once been transparent glass.

The members of the mess were already seated: a smoky vapour arising from the steam of the dishes, which was unable to effect its escape, in consequence of the lowness of the decks, enveloped the busy group. At the head of the table sat a pale, calculating, anxious-looking, middle-aged man, whose sole pretension to anything like uniform consisted in wearing a cross-anchor button on a plain blue coat. A short bull-headed black boy attended behind the president's chair, whom the reader has already recognised as the purser. At the foot sat the officer of marines, whose easy contented air and portly person formed a lively contrast with the meagre figure at the head, who appeared conjointly with him to rule the roast at table. . . .

Bruno, the second, and third lieutenants, both young men of an agreeable exterior, the master, a broad North Shieldsman; one of the "young gentlemen" (a venerable mid, about forty), the surgeon, and myself constituted the dinner party. The first lieutenant sat nearest the door, to be, as he termed it, "ready for a bolt," and evinced great impatience for his dinner. Perceiving the officer of marines loosening his sash to prepare for ground-tier stowage, he gruffly exclaimed, "d—n your belly-band, soldier! bear a-hand and bale out the soup—think every one an 'idler' like yourself?" This appellation I soon perceived, from his alacrity in cutting and hewing down everything edible within his reach, was altogether inapplicable to our good-humoured vice.

The Naval Sketch Book. By an Officer of Rank. (Second edition. London, 1826. Henry Colburn.)

———————•———————

. . . it will be but apropos to say a word of the gentlemen who sat round the table, beginning with the first lieutenant, who was a very good fellow in the main, and a great dandy; did not stand on trifles, that is to say he *started* or flogged a man with a rope's end till he was half dead, ordered a mid to the masthead for four hours, or twenty-four; then a man into irons; the bom-boat woman to be searched for gin; the top-masts and yards to be struck or got up; hammocks or decks washed, and running down the ladder, all in the same breath; sit down to breakfast and renew some argument with one of his messmates, without the slightest emotion; or ask the steward, if he was rather late, why the devil the kettle had not been kept hot? With a hint, that he might *see the gun* before long, "bl—t his eyes!" With his messmates he was a "devilish good fellow," never refused leave to go on shore, took a joke as he gave one, nor assumed any authority (once below) more than themselves; so that the marine officer (the youngest and last as to consequence) was indeed, being something of a wit, the hardest on him in a quizzing match, and his rival to boot, with a fair lady of great virtue and accomplishments, not a hundred miles from Southsea Common.

The Navy at Home. (London, 1831. William Marsh.)

———————•———————

"Mr. Reefknot was the master of the frigate. He was rough and rugged as the Diamond rock, and equally as hard-hearted. He had no compassion for friend or foe, and had completely got on the blind side of the homeward-bound October convoy, during a middle watch, by dousing the light, and altering the course, thereby giving the crews of about twenty sail of merchant vessels, bound from Newfoundland for England, the enviable opportunity of working their own days' works the remainder of the voyage home, should they have the good fortune to escape the acquaintance of some of the enemy's cruisers."

"Did the Captain of the frigate know of this?"

"Certainly not—how could he?—when he went to bed at eight o'clock every night, and took a regular marine officer's round until eight next morning; the more particularly so to show his independence of all control, because the Admiralty had thought fit to appoint him the protector of that part of our nation's commerce on the high seas, a duty far more fatiguing, when attended to, than profitable.

"Mr. Reefknot was a perfect *toady* to his commander, although he disliked him, and had so far won upon the nature of his superior officer that the frigate was entrusted solely to the navigation of the master, who, by hauling up a couple of points, and signing a false log-board, made sure of getting into the track of some prize, which would, to use his own words, help to pay his arrears of mess account on his arrival at Plymouth. Mr. Reefknot was a soaker, and owed the purser of the ship, Mr. Screwtar, both money and ill-will: the former for over-allowance of grog, and the latter for expecting to be paid for it. . . ."

The Saucy Jack. By a Blue Jacket. Vol. I. (London, 1840. Richard Bentley.)

———————◆———————

. . . Of the blue coats, the *purser* brought up the rear; a very sly, demure, correct, calculating fish, excessively grave and slow of speech—indefatigable at his books, by which he made, by hook or crook, some four hundred a year—there being no visible means was of no consequence. —These said ways and means were only known to himself, indeed they were to an active mind in its vocation, like his, infinite. . . .

It must not be supposed that the purser, Mr. Sligh (or Sly as the mids would have it) indulged himself immoderately, as did his friend Mr. Clerk Toby, in the pleasures of the bottle—by no means, on the contrary, it was the theme of many kind remonstrances on his part towards this tallyer and balancer of *books*—no, it was like his whole personal and worldly economy, a matter of nice calculation not to go beyond a slight fuddle after dinner; the quantity was regulated to a glass—so many (all he could get) at the mess-table—so many, from his own private locker (always well furnished by the wine-merchant of whom he got the mess wine), for he had been so kind . . . to accept the ungracious and troublesome office of *caterer of the mess.*

But what may not a man accomplish by attention and industry! Not even this increase of book-keeping (truly, by double entry as the balance somehow or other was always against the mess Dr.) in the least wearied the indefatigable Sly.

[He often declared] with tears in his eyes, how distressed he was at the extreme dearness of every living thing, such as ducks, geese, lambs, sheep, fowls, and that indeed he was almost ashamed of the lengthy bill of those "rascals on shore"; but there was no help for it. God knew!

how scrupulous he was, that the books were balanced to a farthing, and that he had nothing for it, nothing but his trouble, as indeed, he would scorn any other remuneration.

The Navy at Home. (London, 1831. William Marsh.)

In the early nineteenth century, as to-day, a long sick-list was apt to be regarded as a symptom of incompetence. If many seamen were reported sick, it must be the fault of the captain, or the surgeon, or both. The fallacy in this reasoning is obvious. For the numbers reported depended not only on the amount of sickness on board, but also on the definition of sickness to which the surgeon and captain might agree. The list could always be shortened by a refusal to admit that some of the men were ill. It was always to the surgeon's advantage to cut down the number of his patients in this way, as this was a sure means of gaining the captain's favour. Naval surgeons were apt, therefore, to become specialists in the art of detecting "sham-Abrahams," that is to say, malingerers. The readiest means of doing this was to make all treatment uniformly unpleasant. One story was told of a surgeon who treated all his patients with sea-water. When he happened to fall overboard, it was reported to the captain that the surgeon had been drowned in his medicine chest. There were many similar stories, and in most of them the assumption was that captain and surgeon were always in league to limit the length of the sick-list—usually to a standard number, such as a dozen, varying perhaps a little according to the time of the year. There can be little doubt that these legends had a basis of truth.

As the surgeon never would allow more than a certain number on the sick-list at one time, the consequence was, that when that number was complete, any application, however urgent, was answered by: "You be d——'d, I wont have any more on the sick-list to-day"; and often again and again the seamen would be heard to say, "Come, Jack, bear a hand out of the sick-list, it's my turn next." By this means, the ship always appeared by the returns to be healthy: whether this was right is another question.

If a poor fellow presented himself with a long and pitiful face, the doctor, before he felt his pulse, used to say: "You are a cursed skulker! I know you of old—no sham-Abrahams with me; go to the devil, you rascal! I won't hear a word!" And if, by dint of persuasion, he looked at the man's tongue, he always got rid of him by saying, "If you are not better to-morrow, you must leave off drinking grog." This prescription acted like magic on every sort of complaint; but the result of the whole system was a complete squeeze; and a fight, on the cockpit ladder, almost daily took place, to be one of the first eighteen, since this was the number to which our eccentric surgeon limited the sick-list in a seventy-four-gun ship's complement in the winter time.

Gentleman Jack: A Naval Story. W. Johnson Neale.
(London, 1837. Henry Colburn.)

———•———

If a surgeon might be reluctant to invalid anyone else, he had real advantages when it came to invaliding himself. Edward Howard describes, in "Rattlin, the Reefer," the efforts of a surgeon to avoid going to the West Indies. In this instance the efforts failed, partly because, of the surgeons who examined him, one at least feared having to go in his place. The survey resulted in a hot argument about medical theory and a final conclusion that the malingering surgeon was perfectly well. The rest of the story is given below.

But he had yet the worst ordeal to undergo—to brave the attack of his messmates—and he did it nobly. They were all assembled in the ward-room, for those that saw him descend, if not there before, went immediately and joined him. He waddled to the head of the table, and when seated, exclaimed in a stentorian voice, "Steward, a glass of half-and-half. Gentlemen, I presume you do not understand a medical case. Steward, bring my case of pistols and the cold meat. I say, you do not understand a medical case."

"But we do yours," interrupted two or three voices at once.

"No, you don't; you may understand that case better," shoving his long-barrelled Manton duellers on to the middle of the table. "Now, gentlemen—I do not mean to bully—I am only, God help me, a weak civil arm of the service,"—and whining a little—"still very far from well. Now I'll state my case to you, for your satisfaction and to prevent any little mistakes. I was lately afflicted with a sort of nondescript atrophy, a stagnation of the fluids, a congestion of the small blood-vessels, and a spasmodic contraction of the finitesimal nerves, that threatened very serious consequences. At the survey, two of the surgeons, ignorant quacks that they are, broached a most ridiculous opinion—a heterodox doctrine—a damnable heresy. On hearing it, my indignation was so much raised that a reaction took place in my system, as instantaneous as the effects of a galvanic battery. My vital energies rallied, the stagnation of my fluids ceased, the small blood-vessels that had mutinied returned to their duty, and I am happy to say, that, though now far from enjoying good health, I am rapidly approaching it. That is my

32

case. Now for yours. As, gentlemen, we are to be cooped up in this wooden enclosure, for months, perhaps years, it is a duty that we owe to ourselves to promote the happiness of each other by good temper, politeness, mutual forbearance, and kindness. In none of these shall you find me wanting, and to prove it, I will say this much—singular cases will call forth singular remarks; you must be aware that if such be dwelt on *too* long, they will become offensive to me, and disturb that union which I am so anxious to promote. So let us have done with the subject at once—make all your remarks now—joke, quiz, jeer, and flaunt, just for one half hour"—taking out his watch, and laying it gently on the table—"by that time I shall have finished my lunch, which, by-the-bye, I began in the cabin; there will be sufficient time for you to say all your smart things on the occasion, but if after that I hear any more on the subject, by heavens that man who shall dare twit me with it shall go with me to the nearest shore if in harbour—or shoot me, or I him, across the table at sea. Now, gentlemen, begin if you please."

"The devil a word will I utter on the matter," said Farmer, "and there's my hand upon it."

"Nor I."

"Nor I."

And every messmate shook him heartily by the hand, and by them the subject was dropped, and for ever.

Rattlin, the Reefer. Hon. Edward G. G. Howard. (London, 1856.)

———————•———————

Reluctance to sail for the West Indies arose from fear of the Yellow Fever which was prevalent there. So far from having found a cure for this, the physicians of the day had not even discovered its cause. The losses in both the fighting services were extremely heavy. That did not mean, however, that all were equally unwilling to go there. For the sickly season which brought death to some would, for others, mean promotion.

"I must confess I am not so much afraid of cold as of fever. I believe, major, you have been three years in this very singularly hot and cold climate. Now, my dear sir, may I tax your experience to tell us which is the better method of living? Some say temperance, carried out even to abstemiousness, is the safer; others, that the fever is best repelled by devil's punch, burnt brandy, and high living. Indeed, I may say that I speak at the request of my messmates. Do, major, give us your opinion. . . ."

"Well, I will not answer the question, but state the facts. My messmates can vouch for the truth of them. Five years ago, and not three, I came out with a battalion of this regiment. We mustered twenty-five officers in all. We asked ourselves the very same question you have just asked of me. We split into two parties, nearly even in number. Twelve of us took to water, temperance, and all manner of preservatives; the other thirteen of us led a harum-scarum life, ate whenever we were hungry, and when we were not hungry; drank whenever we were thirsty, and when we were not thirsty; and to create a thirst we qualified our claret with brandy and generally forgot the water, or substituted madeira for it in making our punch. This portion of our body, like Jack Falstaff, was given to sleeping on bulkheads on moonlight nights, shooting in the midday sun, riding races, and sometimes, hem! assisting—a—a—at drinking-matches."

Here the worthy soldier made a pause, appeared more thirsty than ever, scolded Quasha for not brandying his sangaree, and swigging it with the air of Alexander, when he proceeded to drink the cup that was fatal, he looked round with conscious superiority. The pale ensign looked more pale—the sentimental lieutenants more sentimental—many thrust their wine and their punch from before them, and there was a sudden competition for the water-jug. The marine carried a stronger expression than anxiety upon his features—it was consternation—and thus hesitatingly delivered himself.

"And—so—so—sir, the *bon vivants*—deluded—poor deluded gentlemen! all perished—but—pardon me—delicate dilemma—but *yourself*, my good major."

"Exactly, Mr. Smallcoates; and within eighteen months."

There was a perceptible shudder through the company, military as well as naval. The pure element became in more demand than ever, and those who did not actually push away their claret, watered it. The imperturbable major brandied his sangaree more potently.

"But," said Mr. Smallcoates, brightening up, "the temperate gentlemen all escaped the contagion—*undoubtedly!*"

"I beg your pardon—*they all died within the year*. I alone remain of all the officers to tell the tale. The year eight was dreadful. Poor fellows!"

Rattlin, the Reefer. Hon. Edward G. G. Howard. (London, 1856.)

———•———

The Gunner, in a man-of-war, was a warrant-officer charged with responsibility for the ship's cannon, powder, shot, and gunnery equipment. He was not responsible for training the guns' crews and his action station

34

was in the magazine. Only on rare occasions would he have the chance to fire a gun in action. In a frigate, however, in chase of a weaker opponent, the professed expert might well be called upon. And it would be natural to expect a gratifying result from his experienced aim.

It is always a greater proof of courage to stand fire coolly than to fire. Captain Reud, I must suppose, wished to try the intrepidity of his officers, by permitting the chase to give us several weighty objections against any more advance of familiarity on our parts. A quarter of a century ago there was some very strange notions prevalent in the navy, among which none was more common than that the firing of the bow guns *materially* checked the speed of the vessel. The captain and the first lieutenant both held this opinion. Thus we continued to gain upon the corvette, and she, being emboldened by the impunity with which she cannonaded us, fired the more rapidly and with greater precision, as our rent sails and ravelled running rigging began to testify.

I was rather impatient at this apparent apathy on our parts. Mr. Burn, the gunner, seemed to more than participate in my feelings. Our two bow-guns were very imposing-looking magnates. They would deliver a message at three miles' distance, though it were no less than a missive of eighteen pounds avoirdupois, and we were now barely within half that distance.

. . . the gunner was burning with impatience to show the captain what a valuable officer he commanded. The two guns had long been ready, and with the lanyard of the lock in his right hand, and the rim of his glazed hat in his left, he was continually saying, "Shall I give her a shot now, Captain Reud?"

The answer was as provokingly tautologous as a member of parliament's speech, who is in aid of the whipper-in, speaking against time, "Wait a little, Mr. Burn.". . .

"Your gig, Captain Reud, cut all to shivers," said a petty officer.

This was the unkindest cut of all. As we were approaching Barbadoes, the captain had caused his very handsome gig to be hoisted in from over the stern, placed on the thwarts of the launch, and it had been in that position, only the day before, very elaborately painted. The irritated commander seized hold of the lanyard of one of the eighteen-pounders, exclaiming, at the same time, "Mr. Burn, when you have got your sight, fire!"

The two pieces of artillery simultaneously roared out their thunders, the smoke was driven aft immediately, and down toppled the three topmasts of the corvette. The falling of these masts was a beautiful sight. They did not rush down impetuously, but stooped themselves

35

gradually and gracefully, with all their clouds of canvas. A swan in mid air, with her drooping wings broken by a shot, slowly descending, might give you some idea of the view. But after the descent of the multitudinous sails, the beauty was wholly destroyed. Where before there careered gallantly and triumphantly before the gale a noble ship, now nothing but a wreck appeared painfully to trail along laboriously its tattered and degraded ruins.

"What do you think of that shot, Mr. Farmer?" said the little captain, all exultation. "Pray, Mr. Rattlin, where did Mr. Burn's shot fall?"

"*One* of the shot struck the water about half a mile to port, sir," said I, for I was still at my post watching the proceedings.

"O Mr. Burn! Mr. Burn! What could you be about? It is really shameful to throw away his Majesty's shot in that manner. Oh, Mr. Burn!" said the captain, more in pity than in anger.

Mr. Burn looked ridiculously foolish.

"O Mr. Burn!" said I, "is this all you can show to justify your bragging?"

"If ever I fire a shot with the captain again," said the mortified gunner, "may I be rammed, crammed, and jammed in a mortar, and blown to atoms."

Rattlin, the Reefer. Hon. Edward G. G. Howard. (London, 1856.)

———————◆———————

The boatswain in a man-of-war formerly occupied a position somewhat akin to that of a regimental-sergeant-major in the army. He was a promoted foremast man on whom a great deal depended. To procure a good boatswain was the first step towards making a good crew. In the fiction of the period the boatswain was frequently given a name like "Mr. Pipes." This was on account of the "call" or whistle which was his badge of office. From the second of the two passages quoted below it will be seen that a married boatswain was sometimes allowed to bring his wife on board as a more or less permanent member of the ship's company. In some ships perhaps as many as a dozen women might be carried, all the wives of the older and more reliable petty officers. More often, however, there would be only three or four, and many captains refused to allow any. The three warrant officers, the boatswain, gunner, and carpenter, were all allowed to have cabins or screened-off berths. The carpenter was, in his way, almost as important a man as the boatswain. He had always served a regular apprenticeship as a shipwright. If tradition and legend can be relied upon, it would seem that the carpenter was always efficient and often extremely clever.

36

But the boatswain was a more amusing personage. He was considered to be the *taughtest* (that is, the most active and severe) boatswain in the service. He went by the name of "Gentleman Chucks," the latter was his surname. He appeared to have received half an education; sometimes his language was for a few sentences remarkably well chosen, but, all of a sudden, he would break down at a hard word. . . . He never appeared on deck without his "persuader," which was three rattans twisted into one, like a cable . . . and this persuader was seldom idle. He attempted to be very polite, even when addressing the common seamen, and, certainly, he always commenced his observations to them in a very gracious manner, but, as he continued, he became less choice in his phraseology . . . he would say to the man on the forecastle: "Allow me to observe, my dear man, in the most delicate way in the world, that you are spilling that tar upon the deck—a deck, Sir, if I may venture to make the observation, I had the duty of seeing holy-stoned this morning. You understand me, Sir, you have defiled his majesty's forecastle. I must do my duty, Sir, if you neglect yours, so take that— and that—and that—(thrashing the man with his rattan)—you d——d haymaking son of a sea cook. Do it again, d——n your eyes, and I'll cut your liver out."

Peter Simple. Capt. F. Marryat. (London, 1834.)

———•———

Though he is a "signing officer," it used formerly to be no uncommon circumstance in the navy to meet with a boatswain who could neither read nor write. A tar of this caste, having possessed himself of the contents of a letter which he had received in the usual official form acquainting him of his promotion, was reading it upside down to one of his superior officers who wished him well: upon the circumstance being noticed to him, he thought to account for it—when he replied, "I axes your pardon, Sir; but you see I'm left-handed!"

The Naval Sketch Book. By an Officer of Rank. (Second edition. London, 1826. Henry Colburn.)

———•———

On a tolerably dirty deal table stood, as I have before remarked, one purser's candle, stuck in a bottle, down the sides of which it had been, and still was, guttering most plentifully, from the constant draught; one black-jack, without a lip, and full of ship's beer, or "swipes," represented the beau ideal of what Mrs. Pipes emphatically called "whistle-belly wengeance;" while a tin biscuit basket, which had once been japanned, was now full of hard flinty biscuit. In addition to this list of *elegantiarum*, the said table also displayed one pewter dish, boasting of both *raw* and *boiled* pork on it, a once-red cruet-stand, with parts of three cruets, and a mustard-pot. The stoppers and mouth-pieces, having long since been destroyed, might well have given rise to Jekyll's well-known "Tears of the Cruets."

With regard to the garnishing of this hospitable board, which consisted of three half-rusty knives and three forks: •it is true that these last were wanting a prong, but Fitzjohn almost ceased to lament this deficiency, when he saw with what readiness the amiable Mrs. Pipes converted them to the use of toothpicks. As to plates, in this submarine abode, they were quite out of the question, since every one took a biscuit on which to cut his pork, and varied the flavour of the latter, with a slice from a large piece of particularly unpleasant smelling cheese, which Mrs. Pipes repeatedly wished down the internals of the purser. Nor was that all, since nothing less, she said, would satisfy her, than that a deep-sea lead and line should be hanging to it.

Gentleman Jack, A Naval Story. W. Johnson Neale. (London, 1837.
Henry Colburn.)

———•———

Maul [the carpenter] according to the cognoscenti of the cockpit . . . was a character—a fish of the first water. . . . He was also a mechanic of all work—for to him all work was alike.

Not that he was a jack-of-all-trades! Maul was master of many. Sometimes he might be seen on the skids, performing the part of "top-sawyer"; sawing with might and main the heel of an "expended topmast," or converting a yard-arm piece into "inch or two inch" of "cappenbar" plank. At other times, repairing a midshipman's quadrant; making a model for a jury-mast; chalking out a "cooper" for the ward-room wine; turning a spare wooden leg for the ship's cook; caulking a leak over the captain's cot; veneering a writing-desk for the first lieutenant; or welding, in conjunction with the blacksmith, a heated hoop at the armourer's forge.

Land Sharks and Sea Gulls. Captain Glascock, R.N.
(London, 1838. Richard Bentley.)

———•———

The surgeon's mate, who later acquired the more dignified title of "surgeon's assistant," was often obliged to mess with the "young gentlemen." This was often something of a hardship in that he was usually older, better educated, and more sedate than his messmates. For the same reason he is considered here as one apart from the midshipmen. Surgeons and their mates were frequently Scotch. In the extract given below an account is given of the reception accorded to a newly joined surgeon's mate by those with whom he was destined to live. In this instance he is made to suffer both as a newcomer and a Scotsman. In this early nineteenth century world the Scotch came in for a great deal of more or less good-natured abuse. In one novel a ship called the "Scotchman"—a name which perhaps veils the identity of an actual ship, the "Caledonia"—is given the nickname of "the oatmeal bin"; the legend being that her crew were all "burgoo eaters, from the captain down to the pigs." "Burgoo" was, and is, the nautical name for porridge.

Meanwhile the young and learned doctor went down ladder after ladder, wondering to what depths the bowels of this vast leviathan might descend and, with the descent of each flight from deck to deck, he lost more and more of the precious light of heaven, until at length this finally deserted him *in toto*, resigning him to the sweet odours and illumination of a few purser's dips, which, like rushlights in consumption, were stuck here and there around him at long intervals to render darkness visible.

Struck with dismay at this novel and unpleasing spot, the doctor exclaimed in horror, "Gudeness guide us, sirs! Where are ye taking me?"

"Merely down into the orlop, Dr. Lindsay, that's all."

"The orlop, sir? I was not aware of its locality. Can ye say, then, where is the cockpit?"

"O that—that's another deck lower down; you shall go down there, if you like it better."

"Not at all, gentlemen—not at all—I am very comfortable here—very; that is rather—that is"—ahem! "it does strike me that there is a marvellously peculiar odour!"

"What, sir!—do you sniff it rather strong? Perhaps you'd like the mess bottle of smelling salts?"

"Thank ye, sirs—no."

"Or the lower-deck vinaigrette?"

"Much obliged, but I think I can manage to do without it—that is if you could open one of the windows anywhere."

"Why, Doctor Lindsay, we should have no objection—the only obstacle is, that here we happen to be under water, which might, perhaps, in such a case come in upon us; in addition to which the fact is we have no windows—but we have reached the mess-berth now. The soup tureen is on the table, and that may revive you."

In a moment the doctor entered, and a seat was given him at the head of the table.

"Sir, can *I* accommodate your cocked-hat?" said one.

"Will you permit me, Doctor Lindsay, to relieve you of your sword?" quoth another.

39

The doctor bowed, and at once accepted the spontaneous kindness of his new brother officers—so different from what he had been led to expect and, as he added, "*so* delightful." He gave his hat to the first, who—sat upon it; and his sword to the second, who—thrust it under the table.

Meanwhile, Doctor Andrew carefully spread out the tails of his new uniform coat, cautious to a degree lest he should crease or sit upon it. This his next neighbour observing slily spilt a spoonful of the hot soup on the seat. . . .

The Naval Surgeon. By the author of *Cavendish* [W. J. Neale].
(London, 1841. Henry Colburn.)

———————•———————

The captain's clerk, like the surgeon's mate, was a member of the midshipmen's mess; and, like the surgeon's mate, he was often out of place there, if only through being a landsman. The ambition of a captain's clerk was to become a purser; but in this, as in other careers afloat, there was no sort of certainty. The captain's clerk might be of almost any age. He might be as young as his messmates or as old as the gentleman described below. As a rule, however, he was to be classed rather as an "oldster" than a "youngster."

The next in consequence was the *captain's clerk:* a sort of broken-down tradesman he had been, and what else nobody knew, though there was a gap in the history of his life of twenty good years, which he never touched on; indeed, he was equally mysterious on other parts, for the shopkeeping part of the story was but whispered about. This gentleman was about forty-five, with a dull yellow countenance and prominent large eyes, flabby, shambling person, and grey head: as he had been clerk in a receiving ship, time out o' mind, he was the most knowing *kiddy*, by many degrees, in the berth. . . . He had, indeed, by long habit, and as a fence against disappointment and grief, acquired a most unbounded affection for *grog;* and though every oldster in the berth was equally fond in the main, yet was his attention to the rum bottle the most unremitting and assiduous. . . . It was often matter of dispute whether he liked eating or drinking best. This knotty point never could be resolved, *he* only knew, and the secret died with him many years after.

The Navy at Home. (London, 1831. William Marsh.)

———————•———————

. . . He had served his time under an attorney, and from that situation, why or wherefore the deponent sayeth not, shipped on board a man-of-war in the capacity of a ship's clerk. The vessel which first received him on board was an old fifty-gun ship of two decks, a few of which remained in the service at that time, although they have long been dismissed and broken up. Being a dull sailor, and fit for nothing else, she was constantly employed in protecting large convoys of merchant vessels to America and the West Indies. Although other men-of-war occasionally assisted her in her employ, the captain of the fifty-gun ship, from long standing, was invariably the senior officer, and the masters of the merchant vessels were obliged to go on board his ship to receive their convoy instructions, and a distinguishing pennant, which is always given without any fee.

But Skrimmage, who had never been accustomed to deliver up any paper without a fee when he was in his former profession, did not feel inclined to do so in his present. Make a direct charge he dare not— he, therefore, hit upon a *ruse de guerre* which effected his purpose. He borrowed from different parties seven or eight guineas and, when the masters of merchant vessels came on board for their instructions, he desired them to be shown down into his cabin, where he received them with great formality, and very nicely dressed. The guineas were spread upon the desk, so that they might be easily reckoned.

"Sit down, captain, if you please, favour me with your name and that of your ship." As he took these down, he carelessly observed, "I have delivered but seven copies of the instructions to-day as yet."

The captain, having nothing to do in the meantime, naturally cast his eyes round the cabin and was attracted by the guineas, the number of which exactly tallied with the number of instructions delivered. It naturally occurred to him that they were the clerk's perquisites of office.

"What is the fee, sir?"

"Whatever you please—some give a guinea, some two."

A guinea was deposited; and thus, with his nest-eggs, Mr. Skrimmage, without making a direct charge, contrived to pocket a hundred guineas, or more, for every convoy that was put under his captain's charge. After four years, during which he had saved a considerable sum, the ship was declared unserviceable, and broken up, and Mr. Skrimmage was sent on board of the guard-ship, where his ready wit immediately pointed out to him the advantages which might be reaped by permanently belonging to her as clerk of the ship, and caterer of the midshipman's berth. After serving in her for eight years, he was offered his rank as purser, which he refused, upon the plea of being a married man, and preferring poverty with Mrs. S—— to rank and money without her. At this the reader will not be astonished when he is acquainted, that the situation which he held was, by his dexterous plans, rendered so lucrative, that in the course of twelve years, with principal and accumulating interest, he had amassed the sum of £15,000.

The King's Own. Captain F. Marryat. (London, 1830.)

To conclude this list of characters a brief portrait is given of the captain's steward. Although a very minor personage in the official hierarchy of the ship, he had always a certain importance as the man likely to know the latest news. Through being in constant attendance on the captain, he was apt to overhear much that was not intended for the ears of the profane. He had, therefore, the choice of two pleasures. He could go about looking profound, or else he could impart his secrets to a few selected hearers. These two pleasures he usually enjoyed in turn.

. . . Unfortunately for his self-elevated importance, which was destined from that hour to be completely kicked from its stilts, he was met midway in his journey by the gunner, whom the noise had drawn from his cabin, and who, quite unceremoniously, laying hold of the collar of his jacket, brought him to a full halt, with the old question rubbed down to a familiar, "I say you, Mister What's-your-name, bear a hand and tell us what's the news?" Such a question from an anchor-button was not to be eluded. Making a merit of necessity, therefore, he threw his ready carcase into one of its most finished congées, and, with a face all over smiles, readily replied: "Really, my good, sweet sir, my news is very trifling—vastly trifling indeed; Captain Switchem and I have been so harassed of late, and the dockyard and the admiral's office, with their impertinent commissioners, their clerks, and all the rest, are such a confounded bore, you know." From this flowery and high-flying way of talking, however, he was suddenly warned to forbear, by observing in the gunner's countenance something of a squall beginning to be apparent, which he dreaded might be yet more obstreperous than the one he had already endured. Making, therefore, a sudden eddy in his speech, he more modestly resumed, "But it can't be shore news a gemman of your rank wants—certainly not. Excuse me, sir; but I'se been in such a flurry all this here morning, that I purtest my poor brain is gone quite a wool-gathering. I certainly presumed, sir—I crave pardon, sir, I meant—I—I understand you to say, as how you wished I to say, as to when we should sail?"

"To be sure I did, Mister Consequence," growled the gunner, highly displeased. "Why, what a shuffling, beat-the-bush knave you are; you didn't suppose I would ask *you* for any other news, did you?"

"Certainly not, my dear Mr. Fireball; to be sure and certain not, sir," cried the still smiling lackey, with a face reddening between shame and rage, at the power which thus rudely and publicly insulted him. "Well, sir, as I was saying, I heard Captain Switchem say to the pilot, in the dockyard there, just before he and I came off, you knows, and just when they parted, says he, 'Bear a hand, Mr. Tackabout,' says the captain, 'for I am quite impatient to be off,' says he. Well, sir, the pilot he answers the captain directly, and, says he, 'I shall merely take a morsel of breakfast, sir, and be with you ere you know what you're about. Just get you all ready,' says the pilot, 'for I'll board you in an hour at farthest, and by that time it will be very nearly flood'; and so, sir, with that Captain Switchem seemed satisfied, and so the gig shoved off, sir, and so—I believe, that's all, sir. But, my stars and garters! the captain will be cross and out of patience at my terrible absence! and me all his things to brush and put away! I assure you, sir, I heard no more, sir"; and with another congée, more stylish than the first, away tripped the grinning domestic, followed by the eyes of the gunner, whose expressive and weather-beaten countenance betokened a something between good-humour and contempt.

"Hilloah, master," cried his mate, with his large mouth stretched from ear to ear in the form of a grin, "wan't you saying as how we would need a spare monkey's tail for the after carronade?"

"I was so, Jack," replied the gunner, turning away, "but don't you think a cat's one would answer infinitely better?"

"It would so, master," rejoined the half-choked mate, "though I'd be content, for this cruise, with serving its breaching with a whacking dose of broomstick."

The Man-o'-War's-Man. By Bill Truck, senior boatswain of the Royal College of Greenwich. (London, 1843. William Blackwood and Sons.)

It is only fair to add that there were Captains' stewards of a different type, devoted, trustworthy and discreet. Servants of this kind would follow their master from ship to ship and then follow him, very likely, on shore and eventually in retirement. One of these makes an appearance in Sailors and Saints by Captain Glascock (see pages 102-103). About another servant Captain Chamier built up his novel entitled Ben Brace. But the historical Tom Allen, upon whom he bases the story, seems to have fallen short of the ideal in a number of respects. And his predecessor in Nelson's service, Frank Lepée, was even less satisfactory.

CHAPTER III

THE MIDSHIPMEN

*The word "midshipmen" is used to head this chapter because it is a word
nerally known and understood. It would have been more exact to employ
e expression "Young Gentlemen" or even "Youngsters." For the indivi-
ials who would now be described as midshipmen then fell into three
tegories, all of which could be comprised by the term "Young Gentlemen"
d by no other term. The youngest boys, in the lowest category, were
ficially rated as volunteers of the first class. They had the officers'
ivilege of walking the quarter-deck but had little authority except when in
arge of one of the ship's boats. They went aloft and might be expected
join in urging the men to greater exertions. Their position, however,
is doubtful and anomalous and every care was taken to convince them of
:ir supreme unimportance. In the middle category were the midshipmen
oper. These had, at least in theory, served afloat long enough to know their
ide. Their promotion from the inferior grade of volunteer was a matter of
tiority alone, involving no examination and, normally, no difficulty.
was a common abuse for captains to enter their own and their friends'
ildren as volunteers while the boys in question were still at school.
nis enabled them to be rated as midshipmen as soon as they went to sea. A
dshipman had, as well as his indefinable position as a prospective
utenant, a definite position in the ship's hierarchy. He was a petty
icer, of higher rank than a boatswain's mate, but of lower rank that the
itswain, gunner, or carpenter. His pay, if insufficient for his needs, was
longer negligible. And his duties and occasional responsibilities were
en heavy. He might act as signal-officer and he might very possibly be
t in charge of a prize. Young gentlemen in the highest category were
ed as "master's mates." Paid rather more highly than midshipmen,
ing men of this rank had functions of correspondingly greater importance.
master's mate usually had a deck allotted to him, for the cleanliness and
ler of which he became responsible. Like the midshipmen, he had to assist
mustering the men at divisions. Although the practice was forbidden, he
ght even act as officer of the watch, especially in harbour. He was more
:ly than a midshipman to be appointed as prize-master. When, as
ietimes happened, a mate in the merchant service volunteered for the*

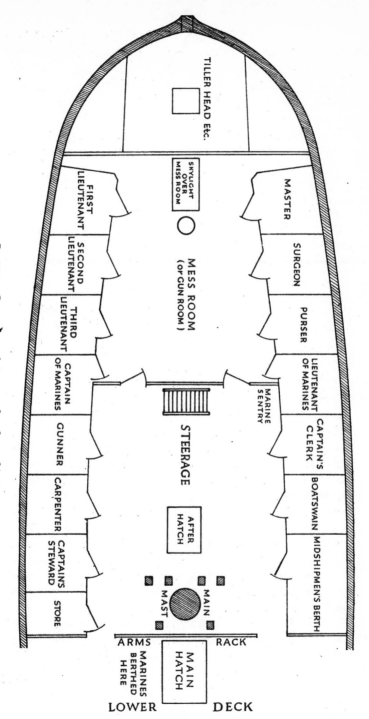

PLATE 3—Gun-room and steerage of a 38-gun frigate.

Within the diagram:

TILLER HEAD Etc.

FIRST LIEUTENANT
SECOND LIEUTENANT
THIRD LIEUTENANT
CAPTAIN OF MARINES
GUNNER
CARPENTER
CAPTAIN'S STEWARD
STORE

SKYLIGHT OVER MESS ROOM

MESS ROOM (or GUN ROOM)

MASTER
SURGEON
PURSER
LIEUTENANT OF MARINES
CAPTAIN'S CLERK
BOATSWAIN
MIDSHIPMEN'S BERTH

MARINE SENTRY

STEERAGE

AFTER HATCH

MAIN MAST

ARMS RACK

MARINES BERTHED HERE

MAIN HATCH

LOWER DECK

navy, he was usually made a master's mate at once. *Ranking, as we have seen, with the master's mates were the captain's clerk and surgeon's mate.*

The individuals who messed in the berth or cockpit were divided, informally, into "Oldsters" and "Youngsters"; and it is important to realise how young and how old they might be. "Young Gentlemen" usually joined at about the age of thirteen. There were instances, however, of boys joining at the age of eleven or even nine. On the other hand, promotion was very uncertain and a midshipman or mate might be of almost any age, some being nearer forty than thirty.

The "Young Gentlemen," however young or however old, had this in common, that they were entirely dependent on the captain's favour. It was in his power to appoint them, promote them at his pleasure up to the rank of mate, disrate, punish, or even dismiss them. There was nothing to prevent a captain disrating a midshipman and sending him forward to serve as an ordinary seaman. It was not unknown for a midshipman to be flogged or sent ashore. Until a man obtained a commission as lieutenant, the Admiralty took scarcely any official notice of him. Even in favourable circumstances, seven years was the probable period of a young man's servitude as a petty officer. For many, this was a period of great hardship. It will be seen that those who entered on this arduous career, although coming from widely different homes and joining for a great variety of reasons, mostly came at first to regret their choice.

Having passed this dread officer [the boatswain], who was just taking a whet or morning dram to keep out the cold, Mr. Tugjunk, followed close by his recruit, advanced beside the chests of the fraternity (placed in rows on either side, outside the cabins) towards the *gun-room* door, where sat on his hams, a sentinel in an undress jacket, armed with his bayonet only—a duty, the rawest of the recruits were placed on, as not being the most particular; being, so as not to lose time, chiefly employed cleaning extra pairs of shoes for those gentlemen who were not provided with a regular valet (on the board wages of a gill of rum every Saturday night). The soldier happened to be thus busy on the last polish of a pair of shoes; but, seeing with great clearness (it is wonderful how vision accommodates itself to darkness, like that of cats) an officer advance, he dropped his brushes with surprising agility, and stood to his arms, drawing himself up, as they passed, quite on the *qui vive*, opening the door for their ingression: and here, beneath a skylight, at a long table placed across, sat all the officers at breakfast, waited upon by the gun-room steward and half a dozen other servants, mostly boys and the valets of their respective lords. Mr. Tugjunk, seizing his charge by the hand, quickly doubled the extremity of the table, and steering him behind their chairs, so as to disturb their worships as little as possible, presented Master Hawser to the first lieutenant, with "here's the youngster, sir, as I brought on board."

The Navy at Home. (London, 1831. William Marsh.)

—————— •◆• ——————

The next character was an officer of an inferior grade, something under that of a midshipman—a floating medium between something and nothing, distinguished by the exalted title of a volunteer of the first class. The pay of this functionary is upon the average about one farthing an hour, taking him sleeping or waking, and that is certainly the cheapest way of making an average of his useful qualities.

His name was Jollopp; he bid fair to be in time an ornament to the service, provided he entirely altered the system upon which he commenced. His father, an eminent chemist in the vicinity of Leadenhall Street . . . [was convinced] that his offspring was destined to be a naval hero. The Lord Mayor for the time being was intimately acquainted with a gentleman who knew the uncle of the captain of the *Rattler*. In the days now alluded to, such a recommendation was often successful; so Master Alexander Jollopp was received on board as a volunteer of the first class. The doting parents of this promising youth spared no expense in his outfit—his sea-chest was divided into several compartments, of divers shapes and sizes, for the reception of case bottles; he had six pairs of striped trowsers, made of stuff very like bed-tick, which cost the tailor some blood to manufacture; six shirts, as many pairs of worsted stockings, and a pair of Hessian boots; a dirk with a brass sheath, and a cocked-hat, were likewise stowed away carefully in the chest. His anxious mother, who superintended his fitting out, in the height of her maternal affection, abstracted from the shop one dozen cakes of palm marine soap, unknown to her husband, and placed them also for the use of her son. There was a mixture, likewise, in a quart case-bottle, which had been prepared by the scientific hands of Mr. Jollopp, for the prevention of sea-sickness, and that was tied up in a cloth to avoid fracture. Now, the chest being too large for the contents, Mr. Jollopp, junior, had the satisfaction, when he uncorded and unlocked it, to find that there was everything uppermost and nothing at hand; and before the *Rattler* had been a fortnight at sea, Mr. Jollopp was left possessed of the case-bottle, with part of the fluid, eleven cakes, and a half of the palm marine soap, and not one clean shirt.

The Indiaman. By a Blue Jacket. Vol. II. (London, 1840. Richard Bentley.)

—————— •◆• ——————

A young man, who goes into the navy in the time of war, does that which is not only excusable, but in some degree praiseworthy, for he is instigated by that insatiable thirst of distinction which is the fever of young blood, and the desire of fighting for a country whose glory is imperishably entwined with the laurels of its sea heroes. This we can all understand; but the lad who goes to sea in the midst of a profound peace, is an unmitigated blockhead, a hapless little ninny, unless possessed of the most irresistible interest, and then, generally speaking, he does not go to sea, but is sent there. But, nevertheless, my brother-sufferers who have been guilty of the same folly, we have this excuse and consolation, we sinned when we were all very young and very quickly repented. I have often thought that it must be the devil himself who tempts all the insular youth of these realms to go a voyaging during their infant years—and this, in spite of all precept, warning, and example. A grandfather who had fought his way up to his flag, and had the satisfaction of dying by the side of Rodney, just as he got the corner of it between his teeth, was wont to declare that a child of his should be put in the fire rather than in either of the king's services: since which, as a matter of course, all three have been despatched in said services by shot, steel, and jungle fever. I, therefore, to make up for the choleric old gentleman's disloyalty, piously intend just the reverse; since one's jocose friends assert that the navy presents the cheapest way of getting rid of a large family at the country's expense. All those, therefore, who in this humorous view consider themselves to have unadjusted claims upon the state, I advise to follow my example for, if your children are neither shot, drowned, nor promoted, they will infallibly take to drinking, and thus either be broken by courtmartial, or dismissed without it; while this gives you the wide and finishing opportunity of "having nothing more to say to them."

The tender-hearted parent, therefore, who has once shipped his son off into the navy, may sit down over his port, and his fire, rub his hands and say, "Well, my dear boy, you're provided for at last." I cannot say that mine took so much trouble, for having written to tell him I was going to sea, he wrote and replied, I might go to the devil—if I pleased. But for all this, he was a very good fellow, and we were much attached—though one would not suppose so.

Gentleman Jack, A Naval Story. W. Johnson Neale.
(London, 1837. Henry Colburn.)

———————•◆•———————

To what it is to be attributed I know not, but certain it is, that among the youth of Great Britain a very strong feeling prevails in favour

PLATE 4—PORTSMOUTH HARBOUR by Thomas Rowlandson.

of a sea life. Robinson Crusoe has certainly something to do with it, and the works of Captain Marryat increase the feeling, by imbuing the juvenile mind with a delusive idea, that an officer in the navy has nothing to do but drink grog, and go on shore and make love to beautiful damsels with dark eyes. The effect of the idea is, to send shoals of the British youth into the navy long before they know anything about their fitness, or unfitness, for it, or any other profession, in consequence of which we perpetually meet with officers afloat who ought to have been parsons ashore, and *vice-versa*. What a splendid boatswain was lost to the service in the Bishop of ——! What a glorious ranter to the conventicle in Captain ——! I fell myself completely into the notion that Providence had intended me for a commodore. I chewed liquorice in the hope that the unwary would take it for a chew of tobacco; abandoned braces, in order to give my trowsers a hitch; and longed for the time when I should have the opportunity of rushing, sword in hand, on some unoffending Frenchman, who had never done me any harm. My guardian offered no great opposition. The navy is a fine profession—and cheap. He was willing to sacrifice his ward to his country: by so doing he would be giving a pledge to the state—in short, getting rid of a troublesome boy at the expense of fifty pounds a year. Besides, who knows how soon a war might break out? I might, possibly, die a hero in the moment of victory—and the cost of my allowance would be at an end, and no funeral expenses to pay.

Biscuits and Grog. The personal reminiscences and sketches of P. Plug.
J. Hannay (London, 1848. Second edition. John and D. A. Darling.)

————•————

Why some youths enter the Royal Navy is a mystery often not easily cleared up; in many cases it is simply because they are youths—boys thinking for themselves, or readily launched by their parents into a life wherein they hope their own child will, by some fortuitous means or superior merit, force their heads above other people's children. Poor, friendless (in a professional sense), in many instances unfit ever to excel, and without the shadow of a chance that good fortune will arrive in the shape of "the fortune of war," they wear themselves and so many as twenty years away in constant subservience and worldly difficulty; they are obliged tamely to see more fortunate men pass over their heads, and perhaps eventually (if neither character nor abilities can be questioned), they arrive at five or six shillings a day, and a small house at some cheap and obscure place, wherein a wife and a host of children must be supported (alas!) in gentility! It is *then* "the shoe pinches" everywhere, and the half-pay lieutenant, whose remaining days are spent in the study

D

of economy and gardening, gradually overcomes his contempt for trades-people, acknowledges to his lady that "nothing is so advantageous as a lucrative business in some prosperous neighbourhood," and condes-cendingly sends his eldest son, Horatio, for whom he failed to obtain a commission in the marines, to a merchant's counting-house in the city of London.

Nautical Sketches. By Hamilton Moore, Jun. (London, 1840. William Edward Painter.)

———————•●•———————

Things were very different in the navy at the period under considera-tion, than now. I doubt much if, in 1809, there could be a greater change in a boy's life than being launched from his comfortable home at thirteen years of age into the stormy elements of a midshipman's berth; for in those days the company was not quite so select as at present; people of all sorts and all descriptions became midshipmen. A shoemaker, who had a long outstanding bill against a captain, cancelled the bill and the obligation by having his son placed on the quarter-deck: hence some of the very objectionable characters, who have in after life so completely disgraced the navy, and men in good society too, who have accidentally met some of these intruders, have formed their ideas of the whole profession by the blundering remarks of a hatter's son and by the awkward demeanour of a tinker's brat.

The Life of a Sailor. By a Captain in the Navy.
(London, 1832. Richard Bentley.)

———————•●•———————

If I were desired to point out the root of all evil in the navy, the secret spring of that tyrannical sway, which has in all societies cast such a stigma on our nautical defenders, I should pronounce it most indubitably to be the result of sending such striplings to sea—mere children.

. . . it is . . . an admitted point, that the proper age to commence a naval life is *thirteen!* This is the extreme verge of propriety with the old school. . . . They are of that age, when, suddenly freed from the restraint of school, they long to start into manhood at once; and whatever they see or hear in others older than themselves, that they do instantly imitate. Thus their education, as relates to the practical part of it, and their bent and disposition in after-life, is necessarily formed and moulded on board a ship. What, let us inquire, is the picture from which they have to copy in a midshipman's berth? In nine cases out of ten—or more—licentiousness and profanity in every shape. No one refinement is indigenous. Here then he learns to swear and drink. He next goes on deck, and meets a first lieutenant of the old school, treating men like hogs, and officers like felons: using language, which many a poor creature whom necessity has driven to live by prostitution, would hold in scorn. He is kept in one continued forced and false dread of punishment. . . . Thus, then, we will say the first three years of a midshipman's life generally passes in skulking his watch, and shirking his duty; and were you to examine ten youngsters at this period, they would be almost wholly ignorant of how to go through the necessary directions in reefing or shifting a topsail, or mooring a ship, or, in fact, of any of these primary and important duties of a sailor; and out of that ten, four at least would be unable to put a vessel about, and to weigh an anchor, and cast the ship's head. Then what can they do? They can drink half a pint of rum, and can carry on "a blackguarding match" with any of the mess; they can cut out to perfection, weather the lieutenant of the watch in a dark night, break their leave, and then spin the first lieutenant a yarn as tough as most folks. But as to their use in any case of emergency, they are no more fit to be entrusted with the lives of the men under their command than a quaker would be. . . .

Cavendish, or the Patrician at Sea. (Second edition. London, 1832. Henry Colburn and Richard Bentley.)

————•————

It is a life, to some, of indescribable misery. How often have I seen a midshipman of forty-five years of age, and a lieutenant of sixty! . . . It will be seen that I was promoted as soon as my age and service permitted. I looked younger than I was—and I recollect poor Preston, when I exhibited my commission, turning round to Sir Alexander Gordon, and remarking, "I say, Gordon, what the devil do the Lords of the Admiralty mean by appointing such boys to *my* ship?" If he had boys for lieutenants, he had greybeards for midshipmen. I was left commanding officer one day, and, being engaged in some occupation below, was informed by the midshipman of the watch that the sergeant had a complaint against the master's mate; what was my surprise to find "a young gentleman"—as midshipmen are termed—of upwards of forty years of age, with a greyhead and weather-beaten countenance. . . . I asked the particulars of poor Steel's life—it was the same as many others: he had been only thirty years in the service—and, having no interest, was likely to be thirty more without promotion.

The Life of a Sailor. By a Captain in the Navy.
(London, 1832. Richard Bentley.)

————•————

In those days in the navy, before we had been polished by the society of females, or enjoyed the benefits of peace, the dinner-service in a midshipman's berth was not quite so costly as a nobleman's. Glass, a brittle material, and one which shows dirt both in the liquid and on its sides, was too expensive and too easily expended to be much used in the navy. Cups would answer their purpose, and therefore cups were used. The soup-tureen, a heavy, lumbering piece of block tin, pounded into shape, was, for want of a ladle, emptied with an everlasting teacup; the knives were invariably black, both on the handles and on the blades; and the forks were wiped in the tablecloth by the persons about to use them, and who, to save eating more than was requisite of actual dirt, always plunged them through the tablecloth to clean between the prongs. Of course, as only one tablecloth was used during the week, on the Saturday it was voted always dirty enough to be put in a bag to await its ablution. The rest of the furniture was not much cleaner: now and then an empty bottle served as a candlestick; and I have known both a shoe and a quadrant-case used as a soup-plate. The sides of the berth were adorned with dirks; and cocked-hats, belonging to no particular member of the community, were placed *a cheval*, like the little wooden god Thor at Upsala, on a ten-penny nail. It was in a habitation like this, "a prison," as Dr. Johnson says, "with the chance of being drowned," and with only one plank between man and eternity that the sons of the highest nobility were placed. . . .

The Life of a Sailor. By a Captain in the Navy.
(London, 1832. Richard Bentley.)

———————•—•————————

. . . His hammock was at length prepared, and the attendant came to tell him so, whilst all the mess hurried out along with him to mark his first awkward attempts at getting into it. Frank summoned all his philosophy to face the task, and waited anxiously to see some one set the example; but all were too wary, and at last he was forced to make the fatal trial. He laid hold of one side and attempted to scale into the canvas folds, but it was all in vain—he merely upset the whole concern, and brought the blankets tumbling on the deck; in his next effort he did manage to climb up at one side, but it was only to rattle over at the other; and his attempts were repeated for four or five successive times ere he effected an actual lodgment and covered up his blushing face in the sheets, whilst his mischievous messmates were leaning convulsed with laughter around him. This one day had been almost enough to convince Frank of his folly; at least it was sufficient to show his madness in one point, namely, in exchanging the tenderness of his mother and of home for the comfortless privations and heartless revelry of a man-of-war. . . .

The Life of a Midshipman, a tale founded on facts: and intended to correct an injudicious predeliction in boys for the life of a sailor. (London, 1829. Henry Colburn and Richard Bentley.)

Perhaps of all the scenes of confusion on the surface of our planet there is none so great as the deck of a line-of-battleship fitting out. The complement of men not being nearly procured, drafts are obtained from the ships in ordinary and from the dockyard. These, of course, are not in such a state of discipline as in a vessel in full trim, and a great deal of noise takes place. The decks are covered with spars, huge ropes, stores not stowed away, tar-buckets, and paint-pots.

When I reached the ship, such was the state of things I found. Stores were being taken in at the lower-deck ports, and guns hoisted in on deck.

"Now, then," roared a lieutenant who was superintending, "blue-jackets, clap on the purchase. (Silence, there, you d——d rascal, will you!) Away you go! That's it, my men. Handsomely the guy!"

"Handsomely the guy!" thought I. "What the devil is a guy? That lieutenant seems the nearest approach to it, visible at present." And so soliloquising, I put my hands in the pocket of my monkey-jacket (for it was March, and bitterly cold in that barbarous Sheerness) and began to meditate. Here I was a helpless unit among a mob of roaring, stamping savages. Involuntarily, my thoughts turned to bright drawing-rooms and warm fires.

"Hollo, youngster," cried the shrill voice of Peppercorn, "stir yourself, come. If I find you with your hands in your pockets again, I'll send for the sail-maker and have them sewn up!"

This was encouraging, so I whipped out my unfortunate paws and began to poke about the decks very busily, the result of which zeal was, that I got in everybody's way, and was tripped up and trod upon once or twice by marines of huge proportions. This damped my ardour a little, but I reflected that everybody had to begin, and consoled myself with the notion, that I would be able to make other people uncomfortable by and by, myself. This consolation, indulged as it is, lies at the bottom of a good deal of what is to be complained of in the naval service. Some other changes must first be introduced before you can abolish flogging!

However, on the whole, I got on very well. I went ashore occasionally with my young comrade, Berkeley, and we made such admirable progress, that, in a few weeks, we were both of us able to discriminate

53

judiciously between the ale at the Fountain and that at the Ship; we held scientific discourse on the relative merits of Cubas and Havannahs; discussed the pretensions of two rival barmaids (one with dark—the other with blue eyes); and at last were both agreed in opinion that Peppercorn was a passionate humbug, and that it was more than probable that Baggles himself was a fool.

And what more, reader, could you expect from a couple of boys of thirteen, sent on board a man-of-war from school, and put under the government of Baggles and Peppercorn? If you are not satisfied with our proficiency, you must be unreasonable indeed!

Biscuits and Grog. The personal reminiscences and sketches of Percival Plug, R.N. (late Midshipman of H.M.S. *Preposterous.* Jades Hannay. (Second edition. London, 1848. John and D. A. Darling.)

The midshipman of the story quoted below, Percival Keene, has explained to a newly joined and very innocent messmate that the First Lieutenant is a Freemason and that the shortest way to his favour is to claim membership of the same fraternity. The fact that Green is not a mason does not matter provided he can make the correct masonic signs. In return for Green's spyglass, Keene undertakes to show him what these signs are.

Mr. Green and I went down to the berth, and I received the spyglass as a present, in due form. I then led him to my chest in the steerage, and, in a low confidential tone, told him as follows:—

"You see, Green, you must be very particular about making those signs, for if you make a mistake you will be worse off than if you never made them at all, for the first lieutenant will suppose that you are trying to persuade him that you are a mason, when you are not. Now, observe, you must not attempt to make the first sign until he has scolded you well; then, at any pause, you must make it; thus, you see, you must put your thumb to the tip of your nose, and extend your hand straight out from it, with all the fingers separated as wide as you can. Now, do as I did it. Stop—wait a little, till that marine passes. Yes, that is it. Well, that is considered the first proof of your being a mason, but it requires a second. The first lieutenant will, I tell you frankly, be, or rather pretend to be, in a terrible rage, and will continue to rail at you; you must, therefore, wait a little till he pauses, and then, you observe, put up your thumb to your nose, with the fingers of your hand spread out as before, and then add to it your other hand by joining your other thumb to the little finger of the hand already up, and stretch your other hand and fingers like the first. Then you will see the effects of the second sign. Do you think you can recollect all this? For, as I said before, you must make no mistake."

Green put his hands up as I told him, and after three or four essays declared himself perfect, and I left him.

It was about three days afterwards that Mr. Green upset a kid of dirty water upon the lower-deck, which had been dry holystoned, and the mate of the lower-deck, when the first lieutenant went his round, reported the circumstance to exculpate himself. Mr. Green was consequently summoned on the quarter-deck, and the first lieutenant, who was very angry, commenced, as usual, a volley of abuse on the unfortunate youngster.

Green, recollecting my instructions, waited till the first lieutenant had paused, and then made the first freemason sign, looking up very boldly at the first lieutenant, who actually drew back with astonishment at this contemptuous conduct, hitherto unwitnessed on board a man-of-war.

"What! sir," cried the first lieutenant. "Why, sir, are you mad?—you, just come into the service, treating me in this manner! I can tell you, sir, that you will not be three days longer in the service—no, sir, not three days; for either you leave the service or I do. Of all the impudence, of all the insolence, of all the contempt I have heard of, this beats all—and from such a little animal as you. Consider yourself as under an arrest, sir, till the captain comes on board, and your conduct is reported; go down below, sir, immediately."

The lieutenant paused, and now Green gave him sign the second, as a reply, thinking that they would then come to a right understanding; but, to his astonishment, the first lieutenant was more furious than ever, and calling the sergeant of marines, ordered him to take Mr. Green down, and put him in irons, under the half-deck.

Percival Keene. Captain F. Marryat. (London, 1842.
Henry Colburn.)

While this conversation was being carried on to windward, two young scapegrace midshipmen were chattering away merrily on the lee-side of the quarter-deck. "Well, George," said the elder, "what will you do when we get into Portsmouth?" "Why," replied the youngster, "the first thing I shall do will be to buy a loaf of soft tack and a lump of fresh butter, and have a good blow out. What will you do, Ned?" "Who! me! Why I have written to my father a long letter to tell him we have arrived, and I shall get somebody to put it in the post office when we get in. I have asked him to send me some money by return of post; if he does, I shall get leave to go on shore, and I will have a cruise as long as it will last."

The Saucy Jack. By a Blue Jacket. (London, 1840.
Richard Bentley.)

THE LAWS OF THE MEDES AND PERSIANS, AS LAID DOWN IN THE LARBOARD OR MIDSHIPMEN'S BERTH.

"Imprimis.—Any member of this mess, who eats a single morsel, knowing that he *dines out*, shall be tried by a court martial for the same, and on the legal finding shall be *firked*.

"Secundo.—Any member who touches the rum, or swallows any portion of the contents of the *grog case* (knowing that he dines out), shall suffer such punishment as a court martial shall in its wisdom serve out."

The Navy at Home. (London, 1831. William Marsh.)

The cockpit messes, in those days, were totally different to the dandy mess-places of the present age. One boy only was allowed to cook and do all that thirteen required; and all day long there was a continued brawl of "You d——d boy, where are you?" In addition to this, those embryo heroes cleaned their own shoes, made their own beds—and, when they dined with the captain, generally had to wash their own stockings—that is, if they could not reef them, to hide low-watermark, as they used to call the black line made by the shoe-binding. Some old hands, long practised in the trade, could take as many as four reefs in, which consists in tucking the dirty part into the shoe, so that the part shown between the bottom of the trowser and the shoe appeared tolerably white. But these were most fortunate rascals! Quite lads of genius in their line.

Gentleman Jack: A Naval Story. W. Johnson Neale.
(London, 1837. Henry Colburn.)

The wicked operation of "cutting down," may be managed in three ways. The mildest form is to take a knife and divide the foremost lanyard, or suspending cord. Of course that end of the hammock instantly falls, and the sleepy-headed youth is pitched out, feet foremost, on the deck. The other plan, which directs the after-lanyard to be cut, is not quite so gentle, nor so safe, as it brings down the sleeper's head with a sharp bang on the deck, while his heels are jerked into the air. The third is to cut away both ends at once, which has the effect of bringing the round stern of the young officer in contact with the edge

56

of any of the chests, which may be placed so as to receive it. The startled victim is then rolled out of bed with his nose on the deck; or, if he happen to be sleeping in the tier, he tumbles on the hard bend of the cable coiled under him. This flooring is much more rugged, and not much softer than the planks, so that his fall is but a choice of miserable bumps.

Fragments of Voyages and Travels. Captain Basil Hall, R.N., F.R.S. First Series. (New edition. London, 1856. Edward Moxon.)

————•••————

At Plymouth we passed our time in the *Caliban* as other vessels dó. At 9 a.m. we went to quarters, mustered, inspected, and dismissed the men. When we went on shore we regaled ourselves in the forenoon on pastry, in Union Street, and spent our evenings at the London. Occasion-ally we would go to the theatre, and on those occasions it generally, by a curious coincidence, blew too fresh to go off to the Sound. Some-times also it happened that we had to pay a morning visit to the magis-trate which generally ended in our contributing a small amount to the revenues of our country. After a little affair of this sort on one occasion, a midshipman of the name of Woggles came on board in that state in which lords wish to be, who don't love their ladies. It was nothing surprising this, on the part of Woggles, for Bacchus was the only Deity in which he believed. The boat came off to the ship, and his form was seen gracefully vibrating on the stern sheets. Peppercorn, who had observed the spectacle from the poop, came running to the gangway to receive the offender—his face glowing with delight at the approaching triumph of his power. The boat came alongside and—shaking the side-ropes—his knees knocking at every step against the ship's side—up came Woggles, his face glowing with the grape. He staggered on board and stood in majestic drunkenness before his commander.

"Good God! Mr. Woggles—you're disgracefully drunk, sir-r-r," cried Peppercorn.

"I be-be-lieve you, my pigeon!"

This was Woggles' sole reply to the indignation of naval power, and he was borne in triumph below.

Biscuits and Grog. The personal reminiscences of Percival Plug, R.N. James Hannay. (London, 1848. John and D. A. Darling.)

————•••————

It was noon, at which time the men and midshipmen dine, and consequently I found my companions at their scanty meal. A dirty tablecloth, which had the marks of the boys' fingers and the gentlemen's hands, covered the table. It had performed both offices of towel and tablecloth since Sunday. A piece of half-roasted beef—the gravy chilled into a solid, some potatoes in their jackets, and biscuit in a japanned basket, with some very questionable beer, formed the comestibles. The berth was about ten feet long by eight broad; fastened seats, under which were lockers, were built round the bulkhead; and the table, a fixture from sea lashings, was of that comfortable size that a man might reach across it without any particular elongation of the arm. A dirty-looking lad, without shoes or stockings, dressed in a loose pair of in-expressibles, fitting tight round the hips, a checked shirt, with the sleeves turned up to the elbows—his face as black as a sweep's, and his hands as dirty as a coalheaver's, was leaning against the locker, and acted in the dignified capacity of midshipmen's boy. Here it is only justice to remark that the occupation of these poor devils' time is so fully engrossed that it has been held by good judges one of the most difficult points to determine which is the most worthy of compassion, the maid of a lady of easy virtue, a hackney coach-horse, a pedlars' donkey, or a midshipman's boy: for my own part, I always gave it as my opinion, which I shall not now retract, that a midshipman's boy in a frigate, having about fourteen masters and no assistant, is about as cursed a situation as the vengeance of man could suggest.

The Life of a Sailor. By a Captain in the Navy.
(London, 1832. Richard Bentley.)

———————•◄►•———————

"Doctor Lindsay," said Taffy, as soon as he had resumed his seat, "I am greatly sorry that on your first doing the *Royal William* the honour to join her, I, the temporary president of the mess, should have to apologise for the state in which you find many of its concomitants. Around you, sir, I grieve to say, you must behold forks without prongs—some wanting one, some even two; plates cracked, dishes without covers; iron spoons with the tinning worn off and tinned saucepans with the iron gone; besides holes in the drinking cups—and, I fear, far too much dirt on the tablecloths; and even I am, as you see, so utterly without a soup-ladle as to be obliged to use a cracked teacup in the place of it. . . . Doctor Lindsay, will you allow me to give you a cupful of soup?"

"Thank ye, sir—that will do, sir—one will be plenty."

"I fear, even here, sir, we must again apologise for the colour of such a liquid. I say, boy," addressing the servant, "you blackguardly,

58

rascally son of a sea-cook, do you call this soup, or the water you washed the dishes in last night, warmed up again?"

The Naval Surgeon. By the author of *Cavendish.*
(London, 1841. Henry Colburn.)

————•◆•————

. . . I soon found my way to the Consul's, and there I saw old Captain Nicholas of our ship, and he read the note I had brought him, and while he was doing so a young lady came into the room. She first looked at me, and then asked Captain Nicholas if I could not remain there a little time, as I must have walked a good way. He said "Yes." Another came in shortly afterwards, and I was then asked to stop to dinner. I said I had dined, but Captain Nicholas replied: "Oh, stuff, midshipmen can always eat two dinners in a day; I have often eaten three myself"; so it was settled I was to remain. I had not expected this sort of thing, and consequently had not taken so much pains with my dress as I should perhaps have done, but Captain Nicholas took me into his dressing-room and got me some water to wash my paws and a towel, and then blew me up for not having a waistcoat on. It is very often the fashion amongst officers in hot countries to wear no waistcoats, but just to button the jacket over. Of course if you are going to dinner you must unbutton, and then certainly it does not improve your appearance—particularly if the ends of your braces are flagged, or, as I have seen a midshipman before now, with a piece of spun yarn rove through the swivel of his braces, and two bowline knots for button holes! Rather nautical, certainly, but not ornamental. . . .

The Navy as it is, or the Memoirs of a Midshipman.
Augustus G. Broadhead. (Portsea, 1854.)

————•◆•————

. . . In our berth we had eight midshipmen, all past the age of thirty, and all, thanks to weather-beaten countenances, copious potations, and disappointed hopes, looking at the least forty. When the news flew round the cockpit that I was promoted, who had only just passed, a loud cry of vengeance was uttered against me. I was scoffed at and reviled; and why? Because fortune had favoured me. . . .

The Life of a Sailor. By a Captain in the Navy. (London, 1832. Richard Bentley.)

CHAPTER IV

THE CREW

The navy of Nelson's day underwent enormous expansion at the outbreak of war, with the result that the peace-time or "regular" man-of-war's men soon found themselves in a small minority. The seamen who had been bred in the service, if of reasonably good character, became petty officers almost as a matter of course. It remained to fill up the lower deck with such men as could be obtained. The obvious recruiting ground was the merchant service, and the more fortunate captains often succeeded in manning their ships mainly from this source, the seamen being impressed at sea or in harbour—as likely as not before they knew that war had been declared. Merchant seamen, however unwillingly they entered the service, were easily trained as man-of-war's men. Not a few of them might have served in the last war, while those who had not needed only discipline, gun-drill, and weapon-training. The officers and apprentices of the merchant service were exempt from the pressgang, but some of these might volunteer—especially after their ships had been left without hands. Even, however, at the beginning of war it proved impossible to man ships entirely with seamen, for many of the merchant ships might be on the other side of the globe. And, as the war progressed and the navy grew, the supply of seamen became wholly inadequate. Landsmen were shipped in increasing numbers until they formed the majority of many a ship's crew. Some of these were tempted to volunteer by bounties and cajolery. More were swept in by the pressgang. Of the youngsters, the "second-class volunteers," a certain number were provided by the Marine Society. The magistrates ashore sent many undesirables to sea as an alternative to prison—or even as an alternative to the gallows. Such deficiencies as remained were made up by enlisting foreigners, negroes and lascars, according to the station on which a vessel served. With such methods of recruitment, it is not to be wondered at if the word "scum" was used to describe a man-of-war's crew.

Among the extracts which follow, some celebrate the qualities of the regular man-of-war's man, his seamanship, his professional jargon, and his extraordinary habits when ashore. When reading them it is necessary to remember that such a seaman, so far from being typical, was by the end of the wars extremely rare. To set against this, the men actually trained in the wars, whether they had begun life in the merchant service or ashore,

*tried to model themselves on these heroes and, no doubt, frequently achieved
a tolerable imitation.*

"Why, you young handsome fellow," he began, as he addressed me,
"are you going to spend your best days with a black face in a collier,
when you might be a vice-admiral of the red in twenty years?"

I looked at him with great delight; it was the first word of encouragement I had received.

"Won't you volunteer for the king's service, my lad?" he continued;
"that's the place where merit is always rewarded, and where the young
and the active get into notice and promotion. Why, I should be ashamed,
if I were you, to spend my life in going for coals and taking them back
again; washing up teacups and cleaning other people's shoes; doing
nothing for yourself and being kicked for your neighbours. Go on board
a man-of-war; be a sailor in reality; make prize-money; laugh and
sing; drink grog, and christen the cat."

I said I should have no objection.

"Objection!" said he, with a stare as long as if I had asked him for
some money or spoken Greek to him; "Objection! why, if you knew
what I offered you, the fortune which I am putting within your grasp,
the pleasure I am proffering, you would fall down on your knees and
thank me with tears in your eyes."

"Oh Lord!" said one of the men near me, "that man would talk a
schoolboy out of his bread and butter."

"Go and look at yourself in a glass, my lad," continued this crimp,
"see what a gallant fellow you would be in a pair of epaulettes; fancy
yourself an admiral, commanding a fleet, surrounded by your officers,
the flag of your enemy just lowered, his sword placed in your hand, your
crew cheering their brave commander, and then look at this dirty
collier, and say, if I slaved for forty years, I could not expect to command
even this."

"I'll enter," said I.

Tom Bowling: a tale of the sea. Capt. Frederick Chamier, R.N.
(London, 1841. Henry Colburn.)

And now, as I have come to anchor after a long cruise to the Western
Indies, I will give my opinion about corporal punishment and impressment of seamen; because every now and then I run foul of a kind of
sea-lawyer, one of the devil's attorneys, and he is always prating to those
who will listen to him, and trying to make them believe that they are,
like dogs, taken, stolen, whipped, and kicked by every man with a pair
of epaulettes, who happens to walk a quarter-deck.

As for corporal punishment then—which means a little back-scratching—I think I may say that it could not be abolished without injury to the service. When the wind is whistling, the rain pouring down, the sea getting up, and the after-guard, main, mizzen top-men, and marines are lugging away at the weather fore-topsail-brace, with their eyes all running over with rainwater, and their tails blowing over to leeward—I say, when it is dark, a dirty, murky, rainy, windy, snowy night, there is many a man who prefers a hammock to a wet jacket. Of course, if these men remain skulking below, the duty will fall the heavier upon the men aloft. Now, it is nothing but the fear of the cat and her tails that keeps such fellows from sleeping, and if you put them in irons, why you only encourage their idleness. You may make them pick oakum, and that's all you can do. You may stop their grog, and they will get more than their allowance from their shipmates. You may clap them in the black list, but that is a bad remedy: nothing breaks a good man's heart more than being mixed up with fellows on that list— and perhaps he may have dozed a bit on the lookout, or the officer of the watch may have seen a stranger before him.

Let them be educated, say some: I say, no, you'll make them worse. Instead of talking of the good old times, spinning a yarn about the Nile, running up one's memory about Nelson, and such like, they would all be squatting about the decks like a set of Turks, with newspapers before them, settling the affairs of the nation, and talking about that which none of them understand! Let them alone; they are used to it, they think less of the disgrace than the pain; and whilst we have officers who are as humane as they are brave we have little to fear from tyranny, and that tyranny can always be stoppered.

Well, then, as to impressment, without being the least personal, I take the liberty of saying, that none of the great people understand the subject at all. Who is to know so much about it as we, who have been on shore, and lugged the man out of his warm bed to make a sailor of him? And, curse their ungrateful souls! some of them try to run away afterwards! as if it was nothing to have board and lodging; to peck and perch at the King's expense; to be allowed to fight their enemies; and to sing a jolly song in the forecastle, when the ship's under a close-reefed main-topsail, rising over the waters like a duck, with as jolly a gale of wind for a chorus as ever seaman can wish: and then, on Saturday night, to have "sweethearts and wives," and to know that

"There's a sweet little cherub which sits up aloft,
To look out for the life of poor Jack!"

62

Well, there are ungrateful people in the world, and we sometimes find them in these pressed men. . . .

Ben Brace, the last of Nelson's Agamemnons. Captain Frederick Chamier, R.N. (London, 1836. R. Bentley.)

I remember one night we wanted some men at the breaking out of the war in 1803 to man the *Victory*, and, as a pressgang was to be sent, I thought I'd go and see the fun. Accordingly, at the time the boat was to land at Gosport, I crossed over in a shore-boat and arrived just at the same time as a magistrate, who was appointed to accompany the gang, in order to prevent any row and to make people open their doors. It was dark and the men were armed with stretchers—pieces of wood just as well in their proper places as flourishing about a man's head, especially if he has not his hat on. The lieutenant who commanded the party was one of your steady kind of men who never makes a noise about anything, but who always gains his point. When we got near a small public-house and heard several voices, he directed his men to stand in such situations as to prevent any escapes; and said he, "Take care you don't use any violence, my lads; but if the fellows won't stop, knock them down." We were all in a regular cut-throat alley, and the magistrate, who said he was a peace-officer, did not like our preparations for war.

The lieutenant and two of the stoutest men entered the house, and the chaps inside soon stopped their singing.

"Who are you?" said the officer to one of the warblers.

"A barber," said he, "and I should like to know what business it is of yours?"

"You are just the shaver we want. Johnson, hand this fellow out!"

"I shan't go for you, or your Johnson either. I'm an apprentice and you can't take me."

"Johnson," said the officer and in a moment the barber was saved the trouble of paying his bill, and handed outside, where he would have called "murder" had not one of the men stopped him by nearly committing the act.

"Who are you?" said the officer to another.

"A shoemaker, *sir*." The affair of the barber had rendered him a little more civil.

"Just the very man we wanted to show our chaps how to cover the foremast-swifter with hide—Johnson—"

"I'm a married man with a family, sir, and I understand you only take seafaring men. My wife will be ruined, and the children left to starve, if you take me: they are dependent on my exertions. I hope, sir, you will consider this, and what she will suffer, poor soul! in her present situation, if you take me on board."

"Ah, you are a civil, well-behaved man; but you have got too many children, and I shall be doing the parish a service by giving you employment elsewhere—Johnson—"

"Shame, shame!" said about a dozen ill-looking fellows. "You shan't take Leathersoles without a fight for it! Come, my lads, one and all! Our only chance is a fair fight; for if that fellow takes one by one, we must go without resistance."

Up they jumped, doused the lights, and made a rally. The boatswain's mate, who was with us, gave a pipe; all of our men crowded sail towards the house, when out went the lieutenant, Johnson, Peters, and myself, followed by these ragamuffins, who had nearly killed the officer, and split the head of Johnson by throwing a pewter-pot at him. Leathersoles fought like a demon; but he got a tap on the skull-cap from one of the *Victory's* men, which made him a bit of an astronomer: for he saw more stars flying about than any man who ever sailed on the Pacific. The rest got away, everyone of them but the barber and the shoemaker; and we were going towards the boat, when a woman, with about six children, came running after us. The little ones clung to the lieutenant, saying, "Oh! save father! save father!" whilst the woman threw her arms round Leathersoles, and declared she would die if he was taken from her. The magistrate had topped his boom directly the scuffle began: he was gone, he said, for assistance, although he never rendered any.

The officer spoke kindly, but the woman would not listen to any reason. "Give me my husband!" she said. "Oh! what shall I do! I shall starve—I shall starve! Sir," said she, as she knelt down to the lieutenant, holding him fast round the knees, "if ever you knew what it was to leave your mother—to be torn from your wife—to be compelled to abandon your children to poverty and the poorhouse, do not be guilty of this cruelty! Leave me my Tom— it's only one man—and look at these dear little innocents, who will pray for you. See, sir, I shall shortly be a mother again. Oh! what shall I do, what shall I do!" and here she began twisting her hands and swabbing her eyes with her dress. . . .

"It's very distressing," said the lieutenant to the midshipman, "very indeed; a most unpleasant service; and in this case, if we had taken the rest, we might have strained a point and released the shoemaker."

"Oh! do, sir, do!" said the woman; and, as she extended her arms to clasp the officer and bless him, a large pillow dropped from under

PLATE 5—Contemporary scale model of a frigate.

her dress. She saw that it was all over, so she caught up her burden and, having got a few yards distant, fired a volley of mud at us. She was one of your regular ladies who act mothers every night of impressment. . . .

Ben Brace, the last of Nelson's Agamemnons. Captain Frederick Chamier, R.N. (London, 1836. R. Bentley.)

────── ● ──────

"You may talk o' the hardships of pressing—your man-hunting—and the likes of such lubberly prate; but if there's never no ent'ring, how the h—ll can you help it? Men-o'-war must be mann'd, as well as your marchanmen—marchanmen must have their regular convoys, for if they havn't, you know, then there's a stopper-over-all upon trade—so take the concern how you will—"by or large"—there's not a King's Bencher among you can mend it. Bear up for Blackwall—ship aboard of an Ingee-man, and see how you will be badgered about, by a set o' your boheaing-hysun-mundungo-built beggars! Get hurt in their sarvice—lose a finger or fin by the chime of a cask in the hold—or fall from aloft and fracture your pate—then see where's your pension or "smart." I'm none o' your arguficators—none o' your long-winded lawyers, like Paddy Quin the sweeper, or Collins the "captain o' the head"; but d——n it, you know, there's never no working to wind'ard of truth."

The Naval Sketch Book. By an Officer of Rank.
(Second edition. London, 1826. Henry Colburn.)

────── ● ──────

We then called at other houses, where we picked up one or two men, but most of them escaped by getting out at the windows or the back doors as we entered the front. Now there was a grog-shop which was a favourite rendezvous of the seamen belonging to the merchant vessels, and to which they were accustomed to retreat when they heard that the pressgangs were out. Our officers were aware of this, and were indifferent as to the escape of the men, as they knew that they would all go to that place and confide in their numbers for beating us off. As it was then one o'clock, they thought it time to go there; we proceeded without any noise, but they had people on the look-out, and as soon as we turned the corner of the lane the alarm was given. I was afraid that they would all run away and we should lose them; but, on the contrary, they mustered very strong on that night and had resolved to "give fight." The men remained in the house, but an advanced guard of about thirty of their wives saluted us with a shower of stones and mud. Some of our sailors were hurt, but they did not appear to mind what the women did. They rushed on, and then they were attacked by the women with their fists and nails. Notwithstanding this, the sailors only laughed, pushing the women on one side, and saying, "Be quiet, Poll"; "Don't be foolish, Molly"; "Out of the way, Sukey: we a'n't come to take away your fancy man"; with expressions of that sort, although the blood trickled down many of their faces from the way in which they had been clawed. Thus we attempted to force our way through them, but I had a very narrow escape even in this instance. A woman seized me by the arm and pulled me towards her; had it not been for one of the quartermasters I should have been separated from my party, but, just as they dragged me away, he caught hold of me by the leg and stopped them. "Clap on here, Peg," cried the woman to another, "and let's have this little midshipmite; I wants a baby to dry-nurse." Two more women came to her assistance, catching hold of my other arm, and they would have dragged me out of the grasp of the quartermaster had he not called out for more help on his side, upon which two of the seamen laid hold of my other leg, and there was such a tussle (all at my expense), such pulling and hauling: sometimes the women gained an inch or two of me, then the sailors got it back again. . . . At last the women laughed so much, that they could not hold on, so that I was dragged into the middle of our own sailors, where I took care to remain; and after a little more squeezing and fighting was carried by the crowd into the house. The seamen of the merchant ships had armed themselves with bludgeons and other weapons, and had taken a position on the tables. They were more than two to one against us, and there was a dreadful fight, as their resistance was very desperate. Our sailors were obliged to use their cutlasses, and for a few minutes I was quite bewildered with the shouting and swearing, pushing and scuffling, collaring and fighting, together with the dust raised up, which not only blinded, but nearly choked me. By the time that my breath was nearly squeezed out of my body, our sailors got the best of it, which the landlady and women in the house perceiving, they put out all the lights, so that I could not tell where I was; but our sailors had everyone seized his man, and contrived to haul him out of the street door, where they were collected together and secured.

Peter Simple. Capt. F. Marryat. (London, 1834.)

The captain of the top, of the watch in which I was stationed, was the beau-ideal of a thoroughbred man-of-war's-man, one of those genuine sons of Neptune whose element is so peculiarly the sea, that, with the instinctive propensities of other salt-water animals, their migrations seldom extend far inland; a fair specimen is rarely to be found so high up as London Bridge, but, to be seen in perfection, must be sought for chiefly within the precincts of Plymouth-dock, or the Point at Portsmouth, where they are, or were before the fashion of queues was on the wane, distinguishable from ordinary tars by a tie reaching down to their loins, of the diameter of a moderate-sized hand-spike. He was one of those smart, active, fearnought fellows, who, blow high or low, scorning the ordinary and safer route by the horse-fly out to the earing, achieve the interval between the rigging and yardarm at a bound to reef or furl, and who exact from those under them a corresponding agility. Although instances of undaunted defiance of dangers the most appalling, so characteristic of the British tars in the ordinary execution of their duty, are frequent enough, yet have I rarely witnessed more striking examples of it than were sometimes exhibited by this man. Among the imperative duties of the seamen, the most trying and perilous are those performed by the top-men; and the risk would appear incredible to many, which, in the common routine of service, these, when mounting aloft in the storm, the vessel rolling gunwales under, and the masts nodding over the side, to cut away a sail, or send down a sprung yard or mast, unflinchingly encounter. I recollect on one occasion, when blowing tremendously hard, and we had parted the main-topsail-yard in the slings, and when the heavy lurching of the ship had brought the two extremities together with a concussion that threatened destruction to any one who should have the temerity to venture out—I recollect seeing this individual poised in the air nearly a hundred feet above the deck, jerked to and fro with a velocity, and retaining his position at the earing, with an equanimity, which excited the astonishment and admiration of all on board. This hero, Bill Johnson, as he called himself, did not allow the grass to grow under our feet. . . .

Service Afloat: comprising the personal narrative of a Naval Officer employed during the late war. (London, 1833. Richard Bentley.)

I found myself domiciled on board the *Rattler*, a fine frigate in the days I am speaking of; she mounted forty-eight guns, and was manned as ships of her class generally were, until they had been long enough in commission to embrace the gradual opportunity of weeding away the riff-raff so bountifully forwarded from Bow Street, Hatton Garden, Marlborough Street, and other places equally respectable, which furnished over-zealous magistrates with the means of evincing their good intentions towards His Majesty's naval service. There is one thing certain, which is, the officers of the ships so manned felt no gratitude for the favours so bestowed, but that, without doubt, betrayed a want of proper feeling on their part.

The crew, as I was saying, consisted of a large proportion of this scum of Britain—a few blackguard renegade foreigners, some half-starved Marine Society boys, a few good serviceable seamen, a few good petty officers, a tolerable sample of marines; and the upper appointments conferred by the Admiralty were of course faultless, as they always must be, because nobody on board dare say nay.

The Indiaman. By a Blue Jacket. (London, 1840.
Richard Bentley.)

———•———

The bluntness, recklessness, and valour, of the English sailor have become proverbial; he is continually furnishing subject for jest and anecdote. Reader, conceive a short thick-set fellow, somewhat about the height of five feet seven inches, with an habitual stoop, a black handkerchief tied loosely round his brawny neck, his legs thrust into trowsers of coarse canvas, a glazed hat, shading his weather-beaten face, and a pigtail of a truly respectable length sticking out over the collar of his jacket of true blue. This is a British sailor, a regular man-o'-war's man, your real Jack Tar. He seldom comes ashore, and when he does it is with an air of contempt for terra firma, which he thinks not at all worthy to be pressed by his "pins."

No man ties on his handkerchief, wears his long-quartered shoes, or chews his pig-tail with such grace as Jack; he is a marine exquisite, the only being permitted to appear at the court of Neptune. . . .

How extravagant are the actions of a sailor on his first coming ashore! He is astonished that the earth does not move and, not finding himself quite right in his "upper works," endeavours to allay his queer sensations by copious libations of grog; then, in company with his girl, he visits the haberdasher's shops, and buys her lace, caps, stockings, gloves, and other articles of finery, till she is completely, to use his own phrase, "rigged out." He must coach it from one part of the town to another, and sometimes has been known to engage a whole stand.

Jack, if a true, thoroughbred sailor, is out of his element ashore, and when his locker is cleared out nothing pleases him better than the sight of blue peter at the masthead, calling him on board again—and on board he goes, his pockets as light as his heart, for no cares disturb the mind of Jack.

The Log Book, or Nautical Miscellany. (London, 1826–7.
J. and W. Robins.)

———•———

To prevent the ship's crew from getting into mischief for want of sufficient employment while running down the trade wind, they were encouraged to come on deck and amuse themselves with various well-known games, such as single-stick, dancing, bait the bear, etc., as soon as supper was over, which was generally about six o'clock; and by the time they had pretty well exhausted themselves, the ladies and officers, with the assistance of the female attendants, would commence dancing quadrilles to the music of Mr. Titterton's flute, on which instrument he played remarkably well. On these occasions, the Captain generally danced with Miss Melrose, while the foremast men ranged themselves upon each gangway as spectators, and endeavoured to admire a species of dancing they could by no means understand—it being so very different from their own, as Jack's pride while dancing is never to move from the spot where he begins to caper, but to step truly to the music as rapidly as he can, moving up and down like a pea blown from the bowl of a tobacco-pipe.

"Look ye, Bill!" observed one seaman to another: "see the skipper; now it is his turn to get under way; there—now he makes sail; let us see if we cannot manage to recollect how he does it—there, you see, he has hauled his wind on the starboard tack; now, he bears up to let that small craft (meaning Miss Melrose) pass without getting foul of him; now he wears right round to get his head on the other tack; see, he boxhauls his partner, wears twice round against the sun, sails round the small craft again, and then drops his anchor under foot. D——n me, if I understand such manœuvring, but I suppose there must be some fun in it, although I can't find it out; but we will ask Peter Moses (the ship's barber) to come and look at them, and then put it down with pen and ink, for he can write, and we will astonish our long-coated gentry by having a genteel caper of our own."

"So we will, Tom," replied the other sailor, "though I think we shall have some trouble in teaching old bandy-legged Bet (the boatswain's mate's wife) to come the rig like a real lady."

The Indiaman. By a Blue Jacket. (London, 1840.
Richard Bentley.)

———•———

About four bells, or 10 a.m.—for matters had been so well managed that there was no occasion for a lower studding-sail to be turned into a screen across the forecastle, as usual on similar occasions—the man at the masthead hailed the quarter-deck, "Strange sail right a-head, Sir, standing for the ship!" "What's she like?" "More like a boat with one lug, Sir, than anything else!" "How far off is she?" "About five miles,

69

Sir," Away strutted the master, whose watch it was, glass in hand, to the forecastle: from thence to report to the captain. "Small boat, Sir, standing towards us right a-head, will be alongside in half an hour; very like Neptune, Sir." Then returning to the quarter-deck, "Forecastle there! get the carriage ready. Neptune's coming on board, and fill the bath there for'ard." "Aye, aye, Sir!"

In less than half an hour the ship was hailed; the usual questions asked, "Whence from?" "Whither bound?" etc., etc., and the sea-god's pleasure announced of his "coming on board."

. . . Neptune received full permission to exercise his sovereignty on board; and spirits having been handed to the visitors on a silver salver, by the captain's steward, the marine deities "wore ship," after receiving the Captain's earnest recommendation to enjoy themselves and the day's sport, but to avoid drunkenness, which might otherwise endanger the safety of the ship.

Jack Tench, or the Midshipman turn'd Idler. By Blowhard.
(London, 1842. W. Brittain)

———————•✦•———————

"Well, the first thing (in course) I does, was to make for old Moses' slop-shop, and search for a suit of shore-going togs. There I was, overhauling rig after rig, just as fickle as a flaw on the sarfis, till I fixes on a white-linen shirt, with a flying-jib-frill, and "throat-seazeing" complete —a pair of gaff-to'sail-boots, and taut-fitting breeks—a black long-tailed coat, towing over my taffel with a skyscraper cape—and one o' your flash-built waistcoats with hanging-ports on the pockets—when docking my tail, and dowsing my whiskers close by the board—I powders my pate and claps on a broad-brimm'd chopper clean over all.

"Well, as soon as I was reg'larly a taunto—everything taut fore-and-aft, and yards squared with Moses. . . . I just takes a bit of an overhaul squint in the glass; then glancing at Moses, who was looking out as sharp as a shovel-nose shark for a Guineaman—"Moses" says I, "I'm d——d, by the cut o' my jib but I'll pass for a parson! Tip us your daddle," says I, "never say die—and scud like a mugen and book us a berth in the mail.". . . Well, at last I weighs, with Moses as pilot—when, after "backing and filling," and boxing about every lane, what led to the coach, we comes alongside her just as she claps on her canvas. "Ye hoye, there, coachee," says I, "what! d——n your eyes, forget your freight?" (for you sees I was "shaking a cloth in the wind")—"Is that your respect for the church?" says I. "Come down from aloft and let me aboard," says I, "or I'll break every lubberly bone in your body." Well, the words was scarce out o' my mouth, when, just as I was

70

stepping in the cabin o' the coach, what the d——l does I feel but a grip by the scruff o' the neck. There I was, all-a-back, boned by the lord, by the Master-'t-arms, and a man-hunting party o' Marines. . . .

The Naval Sketch Book. By an Officer of Rank.
(Second edition. London, 1826. Henry Colburn.)

". . . I was lately paid off from a craft, as was all as one as a floatin' parliament house. There never was gather'd together such a beggarly bunch of pratin' pollytishins. There was the captain o' the maintop as took in the *Times* as regular, ay, as he took his daily allowance. Let the ship go where she would, the newspaper reg'larly followed the feller—"Stead of lookin' after his top, an' the likes o' that, he was always skulkin' below pourin' over papers, or, as was mostly his favourite fashun, readin' out loud to a large, lazy set of haddock-mouth'd listners, the whole o' the parliment-palaver as was cramm'd chock o' block in every column o' the *Times*.—In as many minutes, he'd make as many remarks as ou'd fill a liner's log for a month. There he'd lay down the law—say, if *he* was prime minister, *he'd* do *this*—that the First Lord o' the Admiralty ought to do *that*; if *he* was First Lord, *he'd* know *well* what to do ——"

"Well," interrupted the long forecastle-man, "I only wishes *I* was the First Lord—*I* knows *well* what *I'd* do."

"What?" asked an inquisitive topman.

"*What?*—why, take care o' myself for *life—make* myself *cook* o' the Callydony."

Naval Sketch Book, or the Service afloat and ashore. Second series.
(London, 1834. Whittaker and Co.)

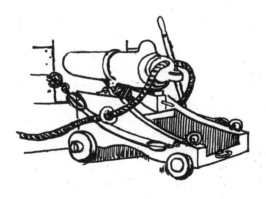

CHAPTER V

THE MARINES

The marines a ship might carry varied in number according to the vessel's rating. Ships of the line would carry a company, and other ships proportionately less, a sloop having perhaps a dozen men and a sergeant. While primarily intended to assist the officers in maintaining discipline, the marines were not exempt from the ordinary duties of the ship. They assisted in scrubbing the decks and in hauling on the ropes. They might have to man the capstan or work at the pumps. They performed almost any duty short of going aloft. Their more military duties included a daily parade, frequent arms-drill and musketry practice, and the providing of sentries to be posted in various parts of the ship both day and night.

The sailors seem always to have felt a certain antipathy towards the marines, as landlubbers and idlers and as men whose characteristic function was in the suppression of naval mutinies. Many marines acted as officers' servants and spent more time in boot-cleaning than in arms-drill. Theirs was an unenviable life. Although immediately subject to their own officers, the marines were under the command of the captain of the ship and were liable to be punished by him in the same way as the seamen were punished. The following extract describes the parade which took place each Sunday forenoon at 9 o'clock.

The guard, consisting of from twenty to thirty marines, who are chosen so as to exclude wardroom officers' servants from taking their turns on sentry each succeeding week, are made to toe a line fore and aft, two deep; and the band at the same time range themselves in a line athwart the break of the poop. The sergeant then goes through the form of making an inspection of their accoutrements, as it is called, after which, reporting all perfect to the lieutenant of marines, he gives the word, "open pans," "slope arms." This is the signal for the lieutenant to make his inspection, who commencing at the drummer boy's end of the front rank, observes to the sergeant, "That this man's hat is not placed square on his head," who immediately orders the corporal to his rear to give it the proper adjustment; a second has perhaps, "too much pipeclay on his coat and not enough on his belts": "That must not be the case in future, sergeant;" another has not used a sufficient quantity

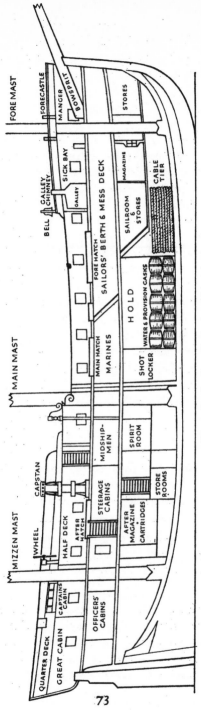

PLATE 6—Section of a 32-gun frigate.

73

of rotten stone to burnish the brass work with which he is bedecked; one has the lock of his musket in bad order, too many rags in his cartouche box, or it may be—the touch-hole of his musket is not clear; in fact any fault found, will, according to the system of the service, be sufficient to show that a *smart officer* is "up to his work." If he cannot discover one in the man's dress or arms, it behoves him, *for the sake of his own professional credit*, to tell him that, "His nose is not straight down the middle of his face," or "His eyes are not of one size." When all have been scrutinised in turn, the orders are given—"Carry arms"—"Shut pans" —"Order arms"—"Right face"—"Examine arms," and three or four more, which when given in a sharp brief style have a very musical effect.

At length after a protracted rattling of ramrods in the barrels of their muskets, and a subsequent examination of them, the inspection is concluded, by orders to "shoulder arms, and front." The captain of marines now makes a concise inspection, and then goes into the forecabin to report to the worthy captain the "Guard is ready to be inspected by him."

Jack's Edition of Life at Sea, or the Jervian System in 183–. Being a series of letters by an old Irish Captain of the Head to his nephew.
(Dublin, 1843. Samuel J. Machen.)

———•———

Dozy was a *galoot*, or one of those raw recruits sergeants are plagued with—and plagued enough had the sergeant been with Dozy, but at last he had drilled him into something shipshape, and bating an extreme slowness of movement which brought his firelock up, when the rest had gone to the next position—his leg behind when it should be before— Dozy was altogether (except when on duty, which he had a natural antipathy to) a sharp fellow, and in his mess was accounted a very dab at pipe-claying a belt, and black waxing his cartouch box.

The Navy at Home. (London, 1831. William Marsh.)

———•———

The following passages show the Royal Marines in a more favourable light. In general, they receive scant justice from nautical writers of fiction. Here, however, is a description of ship's boats about to go on a cutting-out expedition.

The sailors, with their cutlasses belted round their waists, and a pistol stuck in their girdles, or in a becket at the side of the boat, ready to their hands—the marines, in proportion to the number which each boat should carry, sitting in the stern sheets, with their muskets between their legs and their well-pipe-clayed belts for bayonet and cartouche-box crossed over their old jackets, half dirt, half finery—all were ready for shoving off. . . .

The King's Own. Captain F. Marryat. (London, 1830).

———•———

The next extract describes the outbreak of a mutiny on board one of the ships at the Nore in 1797.

The officers expostulated and threatened in vain. Three cheers were called for by a voice in the crowd, and three cheers were immediately given. The marines, who still remained true to their allegiance, had been ordered under arms; the first lieutenant of the ship—for the captain, trembling and confused, stood a mere cipher—gave the order for the ship's company to go below, threatening to fire upon them if the order was not instantaneously obeyed. The captain of the marines brought his men to the "make ready," and they were about to present, when the first lieutenant waved his hand to stop the decided measure until he had ascertained how far the mutiny was general. He stepped a few paces forward and requested that every "blue jacket," who was inclined to remain faithful to his king and country, would walk over from that side of the quarter-deck upon which the ship's company was assembled to the one which was occupied by the officers and marines.

A pause and silence ensued, when, after some pushing and elbowing through the crowd, William Adams, an elderly quarter-master, made his appearance in the front. . . .

"My lads, I have fought for my king five-and-thirty years, and have been too long in his service to turn a rebel in my old age."

The King's Own. Captain F. Marryat. (London, 1830.)

CHAPTER VI
THE DAILY ROUTINE

From the following extracts a fair notion may be gained of the routine duties performed in a man-of-war in the days of sail. It is important to realise that the nautical day runs, not from midnight to midnight but from noon to noon. One effect of this is to cause considerable confusion as to dates for the student of old ships' logs. For the purposes, however, of this chapter, the sequence of routine events is made to begin at daybreak and end at the following midnight. In the first extract a brief account is given of the whole twenty-four hours, but thenceforward most attention is paid to the hours of daylight.

The nautical day commences, either by observation or account, at the sun's meridian, generally supposed to be our twelve o'clock—noon—on shore. At that moment (meridian) the officer of the watch, or more commonly the master of the ship, orders the marine sentinel to turn an half-hour sand-glass (which he has always in charge, and which has been previously run out), and strike eight bells forward: which is accordingly done, and the dinner is piped. No sooner is this glass run out than the sentry calls, "Strike the bell *one*, forward!" and again turns it, when the grog is immediately piped. When it runs out a second time, he again calls, "Strike the bell *two*, forward!" which is no sooner done than the boatswain's mate calls the afternoon watch. Thus he proceeds until he comes to the eighth bell; which is no sooner struck than the watch expires, and the grog is again piped. Previous to this, however, in order to relieve the quartermaster, the helmsman, the look-out at the masthead, and the sentinel at the glass or elsewhere, an individual of each of these classes of the watch below goes to the purser's steward when the seventh bell has struck, gets his quartern of rum unmixed, takes his supper, and is ready, as soon as the bell strikes, to relieve his man with the rest of his watch. All hands now take supper, and, when the bell again strikes, the first *dog-watch* is called. This is only a watch of two hours, and, of course, when the fourth bell has struck, the second *dog-watch* is called, which lasts other two hours, and brings the supposed time pretty accurately to our eight o'clock at night. By this time, however, the hammocks having been piped down, the watch relieved

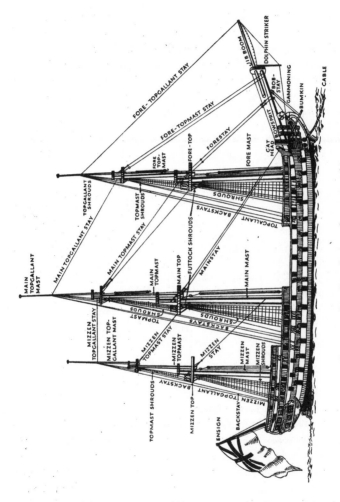

PLATE 7—Standing rigging of a 74-gun ship.

77

generally retire to rest. The watch on deck, therefore, execute all the necessary duties of the ship until their eighth bell has struck, when the *middle watch* is called; and this, again, is relieved, after the same time, by the morning watch, who do the ship's duty during other eight bells, which brings the account of time to eight o'clock in the morning, when breakfast is always piped. At one bell, after breakfast, the forenoon watch is called, who do the duties on deck, while the watch below are scrubbing or fumigating the lower deck, or probably mending their clothes; and thus they continue until a fresh observation of the sun is again taken, and the necessary correction made on the time lost or gained. All this being accomplished, the eighth bell is struck, the day at sea is completed, the glass is turned to commence a new one, the dinner is piped, and the watch called as before.

The Man-o'-War's-Man. By Bill Truck, senior boatswain of the Royal College of Greenwich. (London, 1843. William Blackwood and Sons.)

———————•❧•———————

The account which follows is equally applicable to a ship at sea or in harbour. In the scene described the ship is actually on the point of putting to sea, but the deck-scrubbing process would have taken place, weather permitting, in any case. There was more than a touch of ritual in the outward cleanliness which a man-of-war maintained. The hand-bibles were employed with a truly religious fervour, but more in the interests of smartness than hygiene. It by no means necessarily followed that an equal attention was paid to less visible parts of the vessel. During the French Wars the rage for smartness seldom ran to any absurd lengths. Yards were squared, ropes were coiled, and decks were scrubbed white, but there was seldom much brasswork to polish. The guns, being painted, required no very constant attention. It was only when the fighting was over that the great days of "spit-and-polish" began.

. . . The decks being first well rinsed with water drawn from the sides, and pretty liberally sprinkled over with sand, the holy-stones are next brought forward, and are large flat stones, from 112 to 130 pounds weight—of a soft, smooth bottom, with two iron rings sunk into their upper surface, from which are appended two hand ropes, which the top-men lay hold of, and by dragging the stone to and from one another in the manner of a saw on the sanded deck, they thereby give it a smoothness and a whiteness which the most zealous scrubbing could never accomplish. Small hand-stones are used for those corners where the large ones cannot act upon; and as, in using them, a poor wight must get down on his bare marrow-bones, amid the wet and filth, they have long been known by the cant name of *Bibles*—a term which, by the by, we could remark, *en passant*, is rather inauspicious to the high hopes of those very zealous and respectable individuals who augur so much good from a profuse distribution of the Sacred Volume throughout the fleet, since every thoroughbred man-o'-war's-man must naturally attach to the latter a large portion of that wicked wit, and irreverent contempt, which he invariably feels for the former. The decks being therefore well holy-stoned are once more rinsed with a profusion of buckets of water to carry off the sand, then carefully dried up with swabs, and the work is completed.

As soon as the decks were finished, the top-gallant yards sent aloft, the yards were carefully squared, the fore-topsail let go, a gun was fired, and Blue Peter hoisted—the usual signal for sailing: all which being accomplished, the first lieutenant now ordered all hands to clean themselves, and the breakfast to be piped.

The Man-o'-War's-Man. By Bill Truck, senior boatswain of the Royal College of Greenwich. (London, 1843. William Blackwood and Sons.)

———————◆———————

For the routine duties in a man-of-war, and for her general appearance, the first lieutenant was the man chiefly responsible. The warrant and petty officers received their orders from him and from the other lieutenants. In the more efficient ships especially, the captain's authority loomed in the background, formidable but a little distant. If he wished to interfere, it was usually done in private conversation with the first lieutenant. A captain who took charge of the deck himself lessened the authority of his officers and was rarely well served by them. His direct orders carried less authority than those of a captain whose voice was seldom heard. In the following extract we see the apparently all-powerful first lieutenant becoming sycophantic in the presence of his captain, repeating the remarks of his superior with such variations as might seem to make the sentiments his own. The last of the captain's orders for the day, relating to the astronomical efforts of his "young gentlemen," is better understood when it is realised that "quarter-gallery" means latrine. The pages of learning were to be put to an ignoble use.

It is not every reader that is acquainted with the cabin of a frigate; and it will, therefore, require no apology to take a slight survey of the apartment in which the guests had assembled.

On one side, a row of those *mortal engines, whose rude throats could counterfeit the dread clamours of Jove;*• or, in plain language, four eighteen-pounders, on both sides, turned their breeches on the company. The after (back) part of the room admitted light through the windows of large dimensions, and looked upon the billows curling their monstrous heads, while a bulkhead, or wainscot, forward, divided the cabin from the half-deck.

"The swell," said Captain Brilliant, "is, I think, going down."

"Yes, sir," said the lieutenant, "there is not such a bubbling sea as there was."

"The ship has not much motion."

"No, sir, she rolls very little."

"We will exercise the great guns after breakfast."

"It will be a good opportunity, sir."

"We will fire with the locks, Mr. Hurricane: I have a favourable opinion of them."

"It shall be done, sir."

"Our carronades are warm pieces, and they throw a shot pretty far."

"They are famous, sir, in close action."

Here some person knocked at the cabin-door, and the steward, going to it, returned to the cabin with a bundle of papers.

"The gentlemen, sir," said he, "have sent you their day's works."

"Very well," replied the captain; "put them in the quarter-gallery."

The Post-Captain, or the Wooden Walls Well Manned. John Davis. (1805.)

———————•———————

The following paragraphs describe the several operations of turning out the watch below, lashing and stowing hammocks, and unmooring ship. Where a man was slow to rouse, the accepted remedy was to cut down his hammock, bringing him to the deck with a bump. This was the threat implied in the expression "out or down!" Hammocks had to be lashed not only swiftly but in a uniform style, so as to fit neatly in the nettings, the breast-works in the waist of the ship. "Rigging in dock" was the offence of dressing in one's hammock. The orders relating to the cable-tier and the capstan had the effect of unmooring. The ship riding to two anchors, that is to say, was made ready to sail at a moment's notice. This was done by weighing the best bower or starboard anchor, and then hauling short on the small bower cable until the larboard anchor was right under the ship's bows.

When a ship at anchor had to make sail, the loosing and sheeting home of the canvas and the breaking out of the anchor had to be all but simultaneous. In the scene described below, the seamen are made to scramble from aloft and rush to the capstan. In larger ships it is probable that the marines and idlers were numerous enough to man the capstan unaided.

80

The first thing that saluted the ears of our hero in the morning was the hollow boom of the admiral's gun, almost immediately followed by the boatswain piping, *Up all hammocks, boy!* This command, as usual, opened the throats of all the midshipmen and other petty officers; who, severally, running about the lower deck, exerted the strength of their lungs in bawling, in the roughest notes they could assume, "D'ye hear there, sleepers! up all hammocks! Rouse up, men, rouse up! Turn out there, turn out! Out or down, lads, out or down! Ahoy, you fellow there, no rigging in dock; come, jump! or down you come! Hilloah, who have we got here? Oh! a sick man, is it? Come this way, a parcel of you, and bundle this man of straw into midships out of the way. Pretty behaviour truly! to get sick now we're going to sea— shamming Abraham, I believe? Lash up there, lash up! Move your fingers a little smarter there, Master Whatd'yecallum, if you please! Bear a hand, my lads, and on deck with your hammocks! Come, cheerily, my hearties, quick, quick!" These vociferations, accompanied now and then with a shake of not the most gentle description, had an excellent effect in putting the drowsy god to flight, and enforcing a speedy obedience to orders; so that a very few minutes saw the lower deck cleared and the hammocks all safe in the nettings.

This piece of intelligence was no sooner reported on deck than the boatswain made the air ring again with, *All hands unmoor ship, boy!* an order which was received with a shout of applause.

"Up there, gunner's-mates! down there, tierers! Pass round the messenger, my lads! Carpenters, ship your bars! Stopper the best bower, forward there! Man the capstan!" were now the orders of the first lieutenant, re-echoed lustily, and immediately enforced, by the before-mentioned underlings, who, now that the game was fairly started, followed up the cry with voices in every possible variation of the gamut. "Are you stoppered there, forward?" demanded the first lieutenant. "All ready, sir," replied the boatswain. "Unbit the cable, then." "Ay, ay, sir," was the answer. "In the tier there?" "Sir?" "Are you all ready below there?" "In a moment, sir," replied the master from the main hatchway, "we're clearing away as fast as we can." "Bear a hand then, Stowage, for we're all waiting for you, and the day wears apace." "Ay, ay, sir," cried the master; "I'll sing out the moment I'm ready." "Look about you smartly, then," replied the lieutenant, smiling, "for I care not how soon you begin your song." Then, coming aft to the capstan, he said, "Now, my lads, I expect to see you walk away with her with life and spirit. Not in the dead-and-alive way, mind me, you've lately been accustomed to see on board of a guard-ship, but smart and bravely, like the active service you now belong to. Come, sergeant, where's your fifer? Oh, I see the fellow. Come this way, my little man; stick your body up there, on the back of that carronade, and let's have something lively from you." "All ready in the tier, sir," bawled the master. "Very well, Stowage," answered the lieutenant: "Look out there, forward! Go round; play up, fifer," and away they all stamped, to the favourite air of the fleet, *Shove her up!* amid the cries of "Well behaved, my lads; that's it, stick to her; keep it up, fifer! Surge there, surge; gunner's-mates, look to your nippers! Pay down, my hearties, pay down! Are you all asleep in the tier there? Light out the small bower, will you? Come, another rally, my hearts, and away she goes!" etc., etc., until the anchor was right under, which, after a few cheering and desperate rallies, at length gave way, and was speedily at the bows. While a few of the forecastle-men were employed in lashing and securing the best bower for sea, the capstan was rapidly bringing in the loose cable of the small bower, so that in a very short time it was also right under foot. The first lieutenant now busied himself in sending aloft the top-gallant yards, reeving the royal and other fanciful rigging, then hoisted Blue Peter, and fired a gun as before. The capstan-bars having by this time been unshipped, the messenger tockled along the booms, and the decks cleared up, he now ordered the captains of the tops to see that all their running rigging was in a fit state for working, all which being duly reported, after telling the signalman to keep a sharp eye on the harbour for the captain, the breakfast was piped.

All hands were busied in regaling themselves with their *skillogalee*—a vile oatmeal liquid, in imitation of Scottish porridge—when the boatswain's pipe announced the arrival of Captain Switchem. . . .

The Man-o'-War's-Man. By Bill Truck, senior boatswain of the Royal College of Greenwich. (London, 1843. William Blackwood and Sons.)

———————•◦•———————

The arrival of the pilot put an end to this merry conversation, as the boatswain immediately piped *All hands, ahoy!*—who had hardly time to scamper on deck, when the first lieutenant bawled through his speaking-trumpet the command to *loose sails*, which made the topmen spring to the rigging with redoubled alacrity. . . .

"Fore-top there, main-top there!" bawled the first lieutenant, "are you ready aloft?" which being answered in the affirmative, he immediately sung out, *Let fall—Sheet home!* and away scampered the deck hands with the sheets until the blocks smacked together. "Belay, belay, men!" cried the officer. "Man the capstan! Jump cheerily, my lads. Look out there, forward! Down there, tierers! Are you ready below?" "All ready, sir." "Yo, ho! where the devil have all our hands got to? Foretop there, main-top there! Come down here all of you. Masters Ettercap and Pinafore, kick every soul of them out of the tops—a parcel of skulking lubbers!" "Ay, ay, sir," cried the young gentlemen; and the capstan was speedily crowded. "Look out there, forward!" again bawled the first lieutenant: "Come, my lads, pluck up a spirit, and off she goes. Play up, fifer!" And round went the capstan to a good smart step, the men beating excellent time on the hollow-sounding deck with their feet, amid the accumulated vociferations of officers of all ranks, who, with their potent commander in presence, vied with each other in the notes of alternate encouragement and sarcasm.

The anchor was no sooner run up to the cat-head and fished, than the first lieutenant gave, "Man the jib and topsail halliards—hoist away!" The yards ascended, and the jib ran up its stay, gaily; top-gallant-sails, royals, and skyscrapers followed: and the *Tottumfog*, thus gradually unfolded her white bosom to the breeze, was speedily under way, walking gracefully and steadily through the fleet, in all the glory of new canvas, fresh paint, moderate wind, and fair weather.

The Man-o'-War's-Man. By Bill Truck, senior boatswain of the Royal College of Greenwich. (London, 1843. William Blackwood and Sons.)

———————•———————

In the two pieces which follow, the authors evidently intend a satire on the naval tendency to make too much noise in giving and repeating orders. The sailors were forbidden to sing when hauling on the ropes, in order that the officers could make themselves heard. This was known as the "routine silence." As a matter of fact, in many ships, the carrying out of orders was an occasion less of silence than of uproar. In his "Naval Officer's Manual," Captain Glascock protests against this tendency.

"In the execution of the various duties incidental to the quarter-deck, such as conveying orders, calling side-boys, manning boats, etc., unnecessary noise should be avoided. Hoarse bawlings and shrill screams only impede dispatch, and certainly indicate anything rather than a ship in an orderly state. 'Pipe the cutters away! Boatswain's mate! You, boatswain's mate! Where's the boatswain's mate? Pass the word there below for the boatswain's mate!'

"Such loud bellowings, and privateer shoutings, may manifest pulmonary power; but he who aspires to the appellation of an officer, or desires a ready and prompt obedience, will save his lungs and certainly pursue a more dignified and silent system."

The Lieutenant went upon deck. "Mr. Echo," said he to a midshipman, "send the after-guard aft here, to hoist the main-topsail."

"Aye, aye! sir," cried Mr. Echo, who in concert with half a dozen other weekly-account gentlemen, thus vociferated for several minutes at the break of the quarter-deck: "Boatswain's mate! boatswain's mate! I say, you boatswain's mate! send the after-guard aft here to the main-topsail halliards. Corporal of marines! Send the marines aft on the quarter-deck, to clap on the main-topsail halliards. Master-at-arms! Go down below and send all the idlers up! Send all the idlers up! Do you hear, there, master-at-arms? Send all the idlers up! Stewards and servants, barbers and sweepers, cook's mates and cook-mate's ministers; doctor's mates and loblolly-boys! After-guard! I don't see the after-guard coming aft! Where's the captain of the after-guard? Pass the word there in the waist for the captain of the after-guard!"

The people now came upon deck, the topsails were hoisted, and the walk of the ship was considerably increased. Seven bells was now struck, the hammocks were piped up, and the quartermaster stood at the nettings to receive them from the sailors. And now came upon deck the doctor, the purser, and lieutenant of marines; bloated with eating, drinking, and sleeping.

The Post-Captain, or the Wooden Walls Well Manned. Comprehending a view of naval society and manners. John Davis. (First published in 1805. Reprinted, 1928. Thomas Tegg.)

———————•◆•———————

Shortly after, the helm was put up, for a different destination, to the south, to the great joy of all hands; and from being under topsails, spanker, and jib, as was generally the case—all hands were turned up, "made sail," as if in chase. On which occasion, Hawser was obliged, with many of the other youngsters to scud up to the mizzen top; there to tell the mizzen top boys, what they knew much better how to do, than the said superintending young gentlemen—but they were to learn themselves—which they did, or did not, according to their several inclinations—however, they all joined in the general cry of "Come bear a hand, my lads!" "Are you going to sleep, at the top-gallant masthead?" "Sway away!" "Come, look sharp, look sharp!" "Why don't you let fall?—sheet home!" "I'll come and help you, sir, you d——d rascal, on the weather yardarm!" "Ho! belay!" And while all this was vociferated, fore and aft—the almost hoarse voice, from bawling, of Mr. Shroud, was heard through his trumpet, as he ran backwards and forwards, and jumped about with surprising agility, on the deck.

"Mizzen top there!" "Main top there!" "Fore top there!" "Forecastle there, waist there!" (as it might be). "By G—d you're all asleep. Mr. ——, are you going to sleep, sir? and be d——d to ye!" "The weather royal sheet's not half-home!" "Sir?" "Do you see the weather royal sheet, sir? You lubberly hound! D—n—tion, sir, I'll send you to the masthead for twenty-four hours." "Fore-top ahoy! I'll call you rascals down presently and start you all round!"—then skipping aft, address those below with, "Haul aft—together—why don't you haul! B——t your eyes! haul! you Mr. ——, why don't you make 'em haul, sir?" "Haul! haul! haul!" repeated twenty different mids and boatswains mates' voices!

At last this hubbub of noise and confusion ceased; ropes coiled down, decks swept, and perhaps, some of the unfortunate topmen called down as threatened, and *started*, by way of wind up to the whole.

This was Mr. Shroud's mode of carrying on the duty, having not the smallest idea how things could be quickly done, and well done, without an immense deal of *running about* and *noise*.

The Navy at Home. (London, 1831. William Marsh.)

•————◆•————

It was the chief aim of many naval officers to achieve an all but miraculous smartness in the handling of their ships' sails. This was, and perhaps rightly, considered more important than the smart handling of the guns. Tyrannical captains were known to flog the last man down from aloft. One result of this kind of severity was to produce accidents. It was in the frantic scramble for the deck that men were apt to lose their footing, and sometimes, in consequence, their lives. Inter-ship rivalry was at the root of this obsession, but it must be admitted, nevertheless, that a ship's safety might easily depend on the speedy taking-in of sail, so that this rivalry had, ultimately, its usefulness. In the extract given below, the crew are reefing topsails.

All hands were now ordered aft on the quarter-deck, when the captain, evidently in high dudgeon, thus addressed them: "I am sorry, my lads, that I feel it my duty to interfere between you and your officers; but I will have duty done in a proper manner, and, in my opinion, it's just as well to begin with you as I mean to end. Boatswain's mate, make all the people retire a little farther back, and bring the topmen within the circle." This was done, and the captain continued: "Well, what d'ye think of yourselves now? Are you not a set of smart, clever, pretty fellows? Sailors, quotha! you don't deserve the name! You're a parcel of lazy, lubberly tailors! and move up the rigging like a string of maudling old women or marines. Just look up to these yards, and see what a fine botched piece of business you've made of it. I'll be sworn a bumboat-woman would have done it far better. But I must adopt other measures with you, I find. . . . You must either contrive to do your work better and quicker, or I shall begin to try if I can't compel you. I have got some excellent *cat* on board, very much at the service of every lazy good-for-nothing scoundrel among you; and woe to the fellow, whoever he is, with whom I begin! Away you go, therefore, every man of you, and just do over again what you've already done. You may try, so it likes you, to do it better and quicker; if not, why, I'm in no hurry: we can try it a third time, or a dozen of times, you know—and, with the assistance of the boatswain and his mates, we'll see who'll get tired first. But, avast a bit!—for I had almost forgotten—where is that comely spirit that stuck in the rigging like a French pennon? . . .

The boatswain's pipe now called all hands to renewed exertion . . . but, though the topsails were reefed and hoisted with a celerity which called forth many admirable specimens of agility and exertion, yet had our hero the mortification to find that his labour was as near a conclusion as ever.

"Ah, you lubberly dastards!" cried the captain, who by this time had wrought himself into a frenzy of passion, "d'ye see what a pretty work you've made? Look at these earings, how they're hauled out, you men of straw! and these points, how carelessly and loosely they are tied, you humbugs! Why, don't you see the sail is all abaft the yard together, and fifty times worse than it was before? Lower away the topsails!" bawled he, absolutely foaming: "Away aloft, every lubber of ye, and do it over again. Boatswain's mates, thrash the scoundrels up the rigging! D'ye hear there, forward! Master Marlin, give that careless booby a sound quilting that's asleep with the halliards in his hand. D'ye hear there?" elevating his voice to a scream, "lower away the topsails, you lubber! Move up the rigging smarter, you crazy-jointed rascals! Fore-top, there! come in all of you off the yard. Lie out—reef away! Confound you! but I'll sweat the salt out of your rascally bones."

The Man-o'-War's-Man. By Bill Truck, senior boatswain of the Royal College of Greenwich. (London, 1843. William Blackwood and Sons.)

———————•◗•·———————

The following vivid description of the 'tween decks at midday needs little comment. However unappetizing the food, the time for dinner, and, above all, for grog, was the best hour of the day for the seamen. It was a period of leisure and relaxation, with grog as the great consolation for many ills and almost the sole pleasure within the sailor's reach.

All was now impatience for the commencement of the revels, and every minute was fifty, ere the dinner was piped. At length came the happy hour; and at eating and drinking, with no duty to trouble him, who is so happy as Jack, either ashore or on board? It is no easy matter, indeed, to convey to our readers even the smallest idea of a man-o'-war's 'tween-deck, with all hands at dinner; for the long, loud jolly laugh, the merry catch and cheering chorus—the shrill lively whistle, the ill-humoured boisterous squabble, and the growling deep-toned imprecation—all strike the astonished ear at the same moment with such a stunning noise, that one would think

> "Hell was broke loose,
> And all the devils were there."

As, however, we find it altogether impossible to identify either the speakers or choristers, where all were speaking and singing at once, we have only humbly to propose to any of our readers, whether lady or gentleman, whose curiosity may be so far excited, that they are exceedingly welcome to take hold of our arm while we slowly walk round the crowded deck, and note down the living conversation as it strikes the ear.

. . . "I'se tell ye fat it is, Maister Lillyeuk, or fat-e'er's your name, if thou disna clap a stopper on that vile potato-trap o' yours, d——m me but I'se 'ie ye a clank ower the canopy sall mak your day lights sparkle again, and syne we'll see how you'll like that, my lad. Fa the deyvel d'ye think's gaub to stand your jaw, ye snuffle o' a creature? Confound ye! ye're just a very good sample o' a' the rest o' ye're d——d cockney dirt—aye yattering and yelping when ye're eating, or whan ye've your nose close to the bread-bag!—But bide ye a bit, my man—we're gaun to a place where I'll maybe live to see a hantle o' that cleck o' yours ta'en out o' ye."

"By my soul, you are right, Gibby, and Hollyoak's wrong. I believe we shall see your calf country, my old boy, very soon.—I say, Mack, what d'ye think's the largest tree in Gibby's country?"

"O, how should I know? But what country d'ye call Gibby's?"

"Why, Shetland, to be sure."

"O! Shetland, is it—there I have you, matey, for many's the good glass of grog I've had in Shetland. The biggest tree that I know that grows in Shetland is, let me see, a large, tall, bushy, full-grown— cabbage! Almost as high, by the hokey! as our grog-kid there, ha, ha, ha!"

"Avast, avast there, Mack—Pshaw! you shouldn't be so d——d witty on Gibby's country, my lad, seeing you don't know how much you may be beholden to it yet before you hop the twig. For my part, I'll only say that the man that speaks glummishly of Gibby's country knows very little of the North Sea—I'm certain they don't—eh, Gibby? But never mind them, my old soul; we'll very likely soon be in at Brassay—won't we, Gibby? And then who knows but you'll tell little Ailsey to bring us plenty of murphies, and eggs, and soft tack—Won't you, my pretty Gib? won't you, my heart of oak?"

"Come, come, d——n your squeezing, Jack; my banes are a' sair already wi' your nonsense, I declare."

Here the whistle blew, and *Grog, ahoy!* was bellowed down the hatchway. The sound was heard with a shout of joy; and away scampered the cooks of the various messes with their vessels to the grog-tub.

The mirth grew now both boisterous and tumultuary; the very sight of the grog seemed to have the effect of raising the animal spirits to a higher key; and so very zealously was the carousal commenced, everyone in the joy of his heart talking louder than his neighbour, while ever and anon the rude and boisterous chorus struck the ear, that one would have thought that young and old, in defiance of every caution their captain had given them, were in full march to a state of the most complete inebriety.

"Scaldings, matey, scaldings!—D'ye hear, you fellow? Keep that filthy mop of a head of yours out of my way.—Blast your day lights, you lubber! If you make me spill a single drop of this here grog, but I'll dance your rascally ribs into powder."

"Hollo! you sodger, mind your well-blacked pins, my boy, and don't capsize with the good stuff."

"Number five!—Number five!—call number five below there! Here, my old mate, lay hold of the grog-kid; the hatchway's so completely chock-a-block with lobster-backs and barbers'-clerks, there's no getting down but by the cable."

"Come, come, heave a-head, old skulk-me-ever, and let me pass you: our mess is on fire, mate, and here is the water."

"Weel, sirs! and fat d'ye think o' your fine cockney creature now?" bawled Gibby. . . . "Hang me! if the poor singit mumping cat hasnae lost his call; and ye'll hae obliged to wait till a' the sodgers are saired before ye. . . ."

"Avast, avast there, mates, for here he comes! Come, Hollyoak, hand round, my buck, for we're all in a state of mutiny here. . . ."

"And now that we're all so comfortable, mates," chimed in Hollyoak, a little elevated, "I scorns not to be my share to the harmony; so I'll tip you the fag-end of a Common-Garden ditty, which I've sung with such an applause as you can't think—my eye! It was deafening!

"And shan't I have my vill, old boy?—
    Must ve, dear Emma, part?—
Oh, lauk-a-day! vat vill I do
    To shun a broken 'art?
By jing! sweet gall! a happy thought
    Has just popped in my nob—
I'll go to sea, and fight the French,
    I vill, so help me, Bob!—
So, Emma, love, to heaven above,
    Ven I am far at sea,
Do pray a prayer, and tear a tear,
    All for the loves of me."

"Well, my lads, as I was saying, we had her by this time just two points abaft the beam ——"

"*You* tie an earing, you swab! I wouldn't allow you to stand at my lee-wheel."

"D——n me, if I don't think, somehow or other, that our skipper will turn out a tartar, good weight, after all. He's got a smacking sharp cut-the-wind of his own, and I don't like his top-lights at all, at all."

"Avast there, my hearty; after me, if you please. I say, mates, here's bad luck to Bet of the Jetty, and to all the rascally smouches and humbugs of Sheerness! That's your time of day, my hearts, keep the tot trotting."

"Let us drink and be jolly, and drown melancholy,
    Our spirits to cherish, our hopes and our lives;
For we'll pay all our debts with a flying fore-topsail,
    And so big adieu to our sweethearts and wives."

"Pshaw! d——n the song! hear me out, mates. Well, as I were saying, by this time we were all double-shotted, and were just going to give her another physicker ——"

"Ha, ha, ha! My eyes! twig canny Shields Neddy! Malty, by the Nor'-lights!"

"You lie, you land-crab! I'll walk on a seam with e'er a man of your mess."

"By the powers! You may say it, my darling! For it's just the place for a fellow to laugh and grow fat in. I've seen a good deal now of the world, both east and west, and every point of the compass, honey! but the devil fetch me, were it in my power, but I'd pitch my tent in snug little Ireland before e'er a corner in it at all at all; ay, faith, and so would I now. (Sings.)

89

"If I had, for my share, a nate hunder an 'air,
Och myself wouldn't care, for dull I'd never be;
I'd be off, in a jiffy, to the fair flowing Liffy,
Nor ere roam from home, or I wish you may skiver me:
Hospitality!—all reality!—
No formality there you'd ever see!—
The free and azy, would so amaze ye,
You'd think me right crazy—for dull I'd never be."

The Man-o'-War's-Man. By Bill Truck, senior boatswain of the Royal College of Greenwich. (London, 1843. William Blackwood and Sons.)

———————⸺•⸺———————

It was now a delightful summer evening. The noisy clang of the dockyard had ceased; the lighters and shore boats, with their commodities, Jewish and Christian, and a few unsaleable British beauties, were hurrying towards the harbour; the sun had given to the windows of Blue Town the appearance of a splendid illumination—had tinged the curling tops of the gently rising waves, and the neighbouring richly wooded shores, with a golden hue—and plainly announced to the most casual inquirer, in all the dignity of beauty and expressive silence, that labour must cease, for the day was at a close. The topmen were aloft, and the marines and signalmen were at their posts. Every eye on deck was now steadily fixed either on the admiral's ship, or on the sun, which no sooner sank beneath the horizon, than the words *Fire* and *Sweigh away!* were given, the muskets were fired, the top-gallant yard stripped and hurried with Blue Peter to the deck, the ensign disappeared at the same instant, and the ceremonial of sunset was concluded by the drummer who beat the tattoo to the well-known air *Go to Berwick, Johnny!*

A short interval of order and quietness had now happily succeeded the most boisterous mirth and uproar. The fife, the fiddle, and the drum, with most of their admirers, had gone below; when the pee-wheep-chick-a-chick sound of the boatswain's pipe hurried young and old once more on deck for their hammocks, and a few moments saw the *Tottumfog's* sides, fore and aft, studded with human heads arrayed in all the varied costumes of the world. When all were assembled, the word *Pipe down!* was given; the boatswain's pipe gave its sanction by a screaming trill; the hammocks flew out of the nettings as if by magic, and were as hastily shouldered by their owners, who, in their haste to reach their respective berths below, displayed an apathy of feeling and an equanimity of temper highly exemplary. We have not the least doubt but it would have excited both the wonder and laughter of our readers, to have seen young and old coming literally rolling down the hatch-ladders along with their hammocks; and we have still less, that it would have made many of them stand somewhat aghast, to have heard the strange medley of reiterated shouts of, *Stand from under! Scaldings below there!* and *Murder!* with all the usual accompaniments of mock screaming, peals of laughter, and direful imprecations, which commonly attend this hurried piece of business. All this, however, and a great deal more, passes quite unheeded when once people are a little accustomed to it, for all this is but merely a noise, which a few minutes puts an end to.

The Man-o'-War's-Man. By Bill 'Truck, senior boatswain of the Royal College of Greenwich. (London, 1843. William Blackwood and Sons.)

———————•———————

It has been a custom in the service ever since we had a regular navy, for the sentinel on the gangways to challenge all boats approaching the ship at night. This is done first with a view to prevent surprise and ensure the vigilance of the watch, and next to ascertain the rank of the officer who may be coming alongside. This latter object is effected in so strange a manner, and in language which to the uninitiated may appear to partake so closely of the nature of a secret cypher (if such a phrase be admissible), that its notice may with strict propriety be introduced under the present head of Naval Anomalies. In the first instance the challenge thus comes from the sentinel, "Boat ahoy!"— if it be a captain, the answer will be "Griper," "Growler," or the name of the ship he commands: by this technicality his rank is immediately recognized and preparation for his reception is made accordingly. If it be a lieutenant, the answer to the hail "Boat ahoy" will be "Holloa!" The sentinel then says, "Coming here?"—the reply from the boat will be "Aye! aye!" This at once denotes *his* rank; but, strange to say, in the case of a midshipman, his reply to the first challenge, "Boat ahoy," is uniformly, though most inexplicably, given in the negative, "*No, no!*"

All doubts, are, however, cleared by the answer to the second interrogatory, "Coming here?"—which is in the affirmative, "*Yes.*"

The Naval Sketch Book. By an Officer of Rank. (Second edition. London, 1826. Henry Colburn.)

———————•———————

It was past midnight; the moon, nearly at the full, was still shining brightly. Not a breath of air rippled the translucent wave which reflected her beams, and not a sound was heard save the gentle noise of the tide against the bows of the ship, or at intervals the "all's well" of the sentinels of some distant vessel. All was repose above and below. Our sentries, as will now and then be the case in harbour in the best regulated ships, appeared to be nodding on their posts, and the officer and mids of the watch had either stolen below to solace themselves with the customary refreshment of a middle-watcher, or were tranquilly coiled between the carronades, stealing a nap, or listlessly lounging over the gangway or hammock nettings, absorbed in those waking dreams which the hour and the scene were so calculated to engender. With emotions strongly excited by the events of the last twenty-four hours, I contemplated with admiration the arrangement which characterised the "tout ensemble"—the white and ample decks: those proudly towering colossal masts, the trimness of the rigging, the symmetrical files of those ponderous engines of destruction, bristling forth from her varnished sides; and, when with all this was associated the halo which gave the magic gilding and secret charm to the whole—the proud pre-eminence and well-earned fame of the British Navy—a thrill of enthusiasm made me forget the humble part I was filling in the scene, and dissipated for the moment the depression which my present circumstances were so well calculated to occasion.

Service Afloat. (London, 1833.)

CHAPTER VII

THE FOOD

Every man-of-war was provided with a stock of provisions of a theoretically non-perishable kind, calculated to last any period up to six months. This stock consisted of salt beef, salt pork, "bread" (that is to say, biscuit), pease, water, and rum. There were also minor items such as cheese, vinegar, cocoa, sugar, and limejuice. These provisions formed the basis of the diet. The ordinary fare, however, as laid down in the regulations, could be supplemented in various ways. In the first place, captains were allowed a sum of money to be expended on fresh provisions as opportunity arose. In harbour, therefore, and for a few days after sailing, fresh meat and vegetables sometimes appeared on the mess-tables. In the second place, each mess could purchase such stores as its members could afford. The ward-room officers naturally laid in a stock of provisions sufficient to provide a fairly respectable table for at least a few weeks after putting to sea. The captain usually had his own stock, which was still more luxurious. Sheep, pigs, hens, vegetables, and wine formed the bulk of these private supplies. The midshipmen and warrant officers did the same thing on a humble scale, bringing on board a few sacks of potatoes and other luxuries. The petty officers and seamen supplied their messes in a similar way whenever their means allowed. Lastly, there was always the chance of supplementing the ordinary diet by a timely catch of fish.

In the main, it is probable that the accounts we have of the horrors of a naval diet are somewhat exaggerated. Ships on long voyages and ships engaged in blockade duty often fared badly. Conditions, however, were naturally, uneven. There were men-of-war in the Channel which never strayed far from their base. The ships of the line forming the principal fleets often spent the winter in harbour. When at sea, moreover, they frequently had means of sending for fresh provisions. On foreign stations, even, there might be opportunities to replenish the larder with such unusual items as turtle, rice, tea, or bread-fruit. At worst, however, there can be no doubt that the naval diet could be at once monotonous, insufficient, and almost inedible. Perhaps the worst sufferers were the midshipmen, many of whom had been accustomed to a comfortable home. Invitations to the captain's table and the ward-room were a principal interest in their lives.

93

The seamen admittedly fared much worse, but comparatively few of them had been accustomed to anything better.

There was no reprieve, and, as H.M.S. *Talthorpe* was the smartest ship on the station, in less than twenty minutes we were under sail and passing the *Cymbrian's* quarter.

"Sawyer," said Captain Humbleman, hailing, "cruise between Aegina and Hydra for a week, till you see me."

"Very well. I can touch at some place for fresh beef and veg——"

"Oh! no, never mind that. The master of the transport tells me that your salt junk is very good—two years in cask—only been out in the West Indies once in the *Fly*; but she lost three parts of her crew by the yellow-fever, and so it came home again—no infection, dare say. If you do catch any pirates, you know you can fricassee a few of them for your private table. I'm told they're very good eating—don't vouch for the fact, as Horace Smith makes Cobbett say. Good morning!"—and away we went to sea.

> *Cavendish, or the Patrician at Sea.* Second edition. (London, 1832.
> Henry Colburn and Richard Bentley.)

———•———

The allowance, be it known to the polite world, which England the great—she who gives millions to placemen, and who pensions with thousands the sons, uncles, brothers, cousins, mothers, aunts, and sisters of our cormorant *"secretary birds"* of state—I say this great state, which owns the first navy in the world, and rules the sea with iron thunderbolts, allows to her maritime officers and defenders the following sumptuous breakfast. An insufficient quantity of black tea, of almost the lowest quality, no milk, an insufficiency of sugar—and that a very coarse brown—and biscuit, which not unfrequently is in such an advanced state of decomposition, that it gives birth to animal life. In plain English, you have to watch very narrowly the bread you intend to eat, or the inhabitant animalcules would walk away, house and all, on their backs. Moreover, there is no butter! "Can it be believed?" I hear some of my readers exclaim. "Go to sea and try," I respond.

> *Cavendish, or the Patrician at Sea.* Second edition. (London, 1832.
> Henry Colburn and Richard Bentley.)

———•———

If the food in a man-of-war was often insufficient, the liquor allowed was, on the whole, excessive. Beer was issued during the first few weeks of a cruise, but it tended to turn sour and had to be replaced by grog, a mixture of rum and water. Although the allowance of grog was not sufficient to

94

intoxicate a grown man, it was always possible for a sailor to get drunk by saving up his allowance for two or three days. Drunkenness was the cause of a great deal of indiscipline, which in its turn provoked the savage punishments then inflicted for even trivial offences.

"Vy," at length, reluctantly said Tom Bennett, "I might be a little hazy last night, but I worn't drunk, I know. How could I be? I had only two north-westers," meaning two glasses of grog, half-water, half-spirits, "and a glass due north," meaning all spirits; for the seamen on board a ship mix their grog by the compass points. For instance, due north is raw spirit, due west is water alone: thus, although they may ask for *more northing*, they are rarely known to cry for more westing in their spirited course. W.N.W., consequently, is one-third spirits and two-thirds water; N.W. half-and-half; N.N.W. two-thirds spirits; and then comes the *summum bonum*, due north, or spirit alone, "neat."

✳ ✳ ✳ ✳ ✳ ✳

THE LOGARITHM FOR MAKING PUNCH

As radius is to the distance run,
Is a pound of sugar to a bottle of rum;
And as diff'rence of latitude is to the departure,
So is the limejuice to the water.

Gentleman Jack: A Naval Story. W. Johnson Neale.
(London, 1837. Henry Colburn.)

———————•———————

Recipe for a mess of chowder:—
"Get a clean tin or iron pot, or kettle, if hard up a dirty one is better than none—any port in a storm!—then lay in slices of salt pork, the fatter the better, pepper it well; clap on a layer of shark over the pork, pepper that well; shove in a few midshipman's nuts to fill the chinks, onions or potatoes are better, *if to be had!*—always keep your eye on the corporal 'if to be had!'—then pork again and shark; pepper all separately, and pork, shark, and pepper to the top, within three inches; pour in a teacupful of vinegar, *if nothing better to be had*, and cover all with dough an inch and a half thick. Clap it all standing over the galley-fire, till properly stewed. If you have all-spice well and good; but 'ifs' are bad things in cookery. There are many worse dishes than 'chowder'; so after you have well filled your hide, let a reef out of your waistcoat and thank your God for giving you a good appetite to swallow your whack of a 'sea-lawyer.' Wash all down with a glass of half-and-half, no *three-water grog*, and you need not care to call the King your uncle."

[Note: The shark, or each piece of it rather, was soaked for twelve hours before being made into chowder. Many seamen had a preference for the young shark, sometimes found in the belly of the parent.]

Jack Tench, cr the Midshipman turned Idler. By Blowhard.
(London, 1841. W. Brittain.)

———— •◆• ————

Recipe for save-all:—

"When more fish is caught than can be made use of, or kept without being *spiled*, cut it into slices about an inch thick (Every mess should lay in supplies of whole pepper, dried bay's leaf, and all-spice or pimento— cause why? the devil a shop is there at sea). Wipe the fish dry and lay it in a large jar, as follows: After having pounded all-spice, black pepper, and salt, and mixed it well together, and rubbed the fish well with the mixture, lay the slices in regular tiers; and between every tier a bay-leaf, and so on, 'chock up' to the top, pressing the whole pretty well, or 'handsomely,' and then pour the vinegar down by the side, not the middle of the jar, until the jar is quite full. Cover it over with brown paper, if to be had, if not, a bit of old canvas: tie it close, hand it over to the cook for a quiet corner in the oven, and, when done, lay it by to cool—and there's a supply that will keep till all's blue again. Fine thing for small craft in bad weather, when there's no keeping a fire in the caboose."

"Another time I'll teach you how to make a 'sea-pie' and 'lobscouse.' But pray, younker, what's the difference?" "Why," said Jack, "from what I've seen, a *'sea-pie'* is made *without* biscuit, and *with* a 'dough' over all." "Right, my boy: and 'lobscouse?' " "Is made *with* biscuit in it, and *without* dough at all." "You are a tarnation clever fellow, as the Yankees would say, Master Jack. Many an Admiral could not answer *that* question!"

Jack Tench, or the Midshipman Turned Idler. By Blowhard.
(London, 1841. W. Brittain.)

———— •◆• ————

The capture of a shark is an event of no small magnitude on board a ship. Nature seems to have implanted in the breast of a seaman an instinctive animosity against this voracious creature, something similar to that which the terrier displays to the rat, but the worthy tar carries his hatred and vengeance no farther than the death; for whilst the canine animal, after shaking the life out of him, leaves his victim untouched, honest Jack indulges in gastronomic desires, and like the cannibals of the South Sea islands, actually eats his conquered enemy— for a piece of shark, though rather dry when cooked by itself, may

96

PLATE 9—FRIGATE ACTION.

nevertheless be nicely fried in oil, and served up as a fish steak—if it be amalgamated with savoury things, such as a delicate piece of briny-junk, with a due proportion of salt pork (the yankee is the best), both having been previously towed overboard for several hours, it makes a delicious sea-pie, with as many decks as the cook pleases. Reader, did you ever taste a glorious—full of gravy—voluptuous sea-pie? (I am smacking my lips at this moment.) One of five tiers, magnificently piled up in a camp-kettle? The crusts rich with the juice of the melting viands, and emitting odours that might draw an angel from the spheres? You never have! Well then, before long I will give you full directions how to manufacture this exquisite dainty—but to enjoy it to perfection you must first put yourself upon short allowance for three months; hard, mouldy biscuit, replete with animation, and strongly inclined to run away from you; beef that can be compared to nothing more applicable than pickled mahogany; and occasionally the choice indulgence of cheese, perfectly innocent of cream, but concocted of rancid fat, kitchen stuff, beeswax, and glue, with a mixture of yellow and red ochre to give it colour—as for the fragrance which it emitted after a long perspiration in the purser's store-room—faugh! I had better say nothing about it; but I have actually known purser's stewards so powerfully impregnated by the effluvia that they never got rid of it through the remainder of their existence.

But to return to the shark. Another pleasant meal may be gathered from its tail, converted into what the sailors call chowder; in fact, after a four months' cruise upon ship's provisions, a sixteen-feet-in-length shark is by no means a despicable prize for those who relish a fresh meal.

The Old Sailor's Jolly Boat, laden with tales, yarns, scraps, fragments, etc., etc., to please all hands; pulled by Wit, Fun, Humor, and Pathos, and steered by M. H. Barker. (London, 1844. W. Strange.)

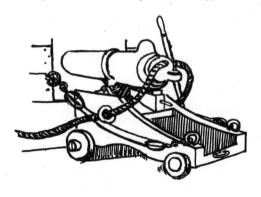

Chapter VIII

IN HARBOUR

This chapter is not concerned with the pleasures enjoyed by the man-of-war's man at Port Mahon, Halifax, or Bombay, but with the delights of the English harbours, Portsmouth, Plymouth, Sheerness, and Falmouth. Of most seaports the nautical opinion was that they were excellent to call at but less so to live in. On a ship's arrival, she was instantly surrounded by a swarm of boats containing provisions and prostitutes. At such times, and more especially after a long period at sea, ordinary bread, "soft Tack," was itself a luxury and butter something to be dreamed of for weeks before-hand. Then there were the taverns ashore, both for officers and men— provided the latter were given leave. The famous Inns at Portsmouth were the George, the Star and Garter, and the Blue Posts, the first-named catering chiefly for officers of rank and the last-named for midshipmen. There was the theatre, the billiard-rooms, and the society of a garrison town.

Except when a ship was paid off, captains were unwilling to allow their men ashore, for fear of desertion. When the men were thus confined on board, it was usual to allow their wives and female friends to join them. Such a ship would be full of women until the time came to sail. The captain and some of the officers would live on shore. both from preference and in the interests of discipline. Some captains, on the other hand, gave leave to their men, so many at a time, making those on board answer for the return of their messmates. Under humane officers, this system answered fairly well. But first lieutenants were relieved, as a rule, to find them-selves at sea again with their crews intact.

If you ask a midshipman which seaport he prefers, expecting perhaps (if you are very verdant) an answer on public grounds, you will hear, that Sheerness is best, because so near to London, or Portsmouth, on account of its hotel, and other advantages (nothing about the dock-yards, or anything of that sort); but Plymouth is not popular, at least, if we may judge from the fact that "west-countryman" is generally used as a term of derision in the service. I, for my part, enter a decided veto against *all* English seaports, as place of residence, on the following grounds:

In the first place, it always rains at Plymouth; always blows at Portsmouth; and at Sheerness, always does both.

With regard to the society of seaports, nobody cares a rap for you unless you are naval or military, and if you are, they care for you in proportion to your money. Ensign Booby, with £800 a year, obtains more respect than any captain or colonel of inferior means. In the next place, if you are single, you are bored to death by mammas wanting to get you married and, if you are married, your wife is probably snubbed by the wives of other people. . . .

And then, reader, the *shoppiness* of seaport social conversation! When military power is dominant, you hear of So-and-so of the 101st and So-and-so of the 180th; how Slugsby's horse ran at the Tweedledum Races; and how Jenkins pulled the nose of Blubber of the Heavy Baboons Regiment; of the prices of saddles and bridles, and the merits of hair triggers; of the late court martial and the new cartouche-box.

Even this is more tolerable, however (with shame I confess it) than the *shop* dialogue of a naval party. There you hear of the *Vanguard's* lower-deck ports and the *Inconstant's* rate of sailing; of hoisting in a launch or rigging a pinnace. There, you, and your wives and daughters, may learn the latest improvements in all naval inventions. Should an elderly lady be anxious to know which clue of a mainsail to haul up when it is blowing hard (a piece of information most useful to her), she is sure to learn it in such societies; and a high-church divine may acquire a perfect acquaintance with the merits of Symondite vessels.

As to seaport *scandal*, I leave that department with confidence till I speak of Malta. . . .

Biscuits and Grog. The personal reminiscences and sketches of Percival Plug, R.N. (late Midshipman of H.M.S. *Preposterous.*) James Hannay. (London, Second edition, 1848. John and D. A. Darling.)

———•———

It was still light when they drove under the arched gateway of the ramparts and entered upon the bustling streets, where blue, white, and gold were the prominent colours; whilst it actually seemed to have been raining cocked-hats, for scarcely anything else could be seen. Officers of every grade were moving to and fro in High-street; but as soon as another gateway had been passed, on to the Point, then the Jack Tars were quietly clustered together, either on liberty, or waiting with their boats at the Sally Port.

This was all new to Ned, and when, on alighting and entering the coffee-room at the Blue Posts, he found it filled with midshipmen, literally enjoying their "tea for two and toast for six," it presented a picture of life that exactly tallied with his own views and wishes. There were youths of all ages, from the child of ten to the young man of twenty-two, wearing the same uniform, and all assuming a degree of independence, as if they relied solely upon their own merits for advancement in the service.

The Naval Club, or Reminiscences of Service. M. H. Barker.
(London, 1843. Henry Colburn.)

———————•◦•———————

Portsmouth Point was—I say was, for I have not seen it these five-and-twenty years—a long street, running from the barriers and drawbridge that separated it from High-street, till it terminated in a shingly beach up the harbour; and being nothing more than a narrow slip of isolated land, from thence it derived its name. There was also a sort of purlieu or by-lane, with an intervening space, which, from its having an old capstan in its centre, was designated Capstan-square.

A noted spot was the Point in the days of war. There stood the inviting "Blue Posts," where many a hungry reefer has enjoyed his tea for two and toast for six. Oh it was a delectable sight to witness the eagerness with which the "young gentlemen" regaled themselves; d—ing the waiters, to show that they were real officers, and topping the grandee in extraordinary style, without the least fear of bring brought up, all standing, by the first lieutenant.

Dear delightful Blue Posts, how well do I remember your characteristic columns at the entrance, and the snug coffee-room on the right-hand side of the passage; happy and joyous have been the hours I have passed within those walls—many a bleak winter morning have I had charge of the large cutter, and pulled or sailed in from Spithead, shivering with cold—wet, hungry, and fretful. Ordered by the hard-hearted and cruel first lieutenant not to quit the boat myself, nor suffer the men to do so; no sooner did the cutter's nose grate upon the beach at Sally-port than I manifested my obedience by lodging the crew at the Duncan's Head (where, as a matter of course, I paid the shot), and then hurrying to the Blue Posts, have found a dozen or more, equally as attentive to duty as myself—luxuriating in the warmth of a glowing fire—sitting over their steaming cups, and swearing big oaths that they would submit to no control but that of the captain: for whom probably a letter lay by their side, with orders from the first lieutenant that "it should be delivered immediately on landing."

"Waiter, breakfast! and bear a hand about it," was the order; and in came the hot rolls, not merely unctuously spread with—for that would hardly have contented a midshipman's palate—but swimming in butter, to gratify a half-famished appetite, and no fond mamma or discreet papa at hand to check their darling in his gorge. Oh, the glorious, delicious,

PLATE 10—Portsmouth Point to-day.

melting morsels; how rapidly were they devoured; and ever and anon the room resounded with the demand, "Waiter, more rolls."

What a history might that place record! How many young and ardent aspirants to naval fame have congregated there in the first opening dawn of their glory—from the child of ten years, who fancied his cocked-hat and uniform made him a man, to the bold dashing middy of twenty, who proudly calculated upon having done "some service to the state."

I can remember many a fine handsome youth, full of eager hope and expectation, longing for the time of his servitude to expire, and reckoning up the sum of influence he possessed to obtain a commission from the hard-fisted, patronage-loving first lord of the Admiralty. There were young men who fearlessly sought danger—

"Even in the cannon's mouth."

and where are they now? Some I see occasionally are greyheaded old men, who, having gained the desired step, have never risen higher; lieutenants who toiled amidst the alternate strifes of storm and battle for some twenty or thirty years, and there they are, lieutenants still, whilst boys—mere boys, who never smelt powder, but in firing a salute, have grasped the coveted distinction, and sport their pair of epaulettes. Others, it is true, are now old-post captains, and some few have hoisted their flag, but the greatest portion have been swept away into the dark abyss of eternity.

But to the Point again. There also stood the "Star and Garter"; but that was more of a lieutenant's house—a touch of the higher grade—a sort of weather-side of "entertainment for man and horse." I frequented it in later days when I crept from under the lee of the mizzen-stay-sail; but though the refreshments were excellent and the company somewhat select, yet I never felt so much at ease, or revelled in such unbounded luxury, as at the dear old Blue Posts.

Jem Bunt: A tale of the Land and the Ocean. By "The Old Sailor."
(London, c. 1845. Willoughby and Co.)

———————•◦•——————

In those times, for we are now in 1801, it was customary for women to be admitted on board the ships; and few can tell, and none can imagine, the scenes which generally followed the admission of these degraded creatures—drunkenness was the lightest offence against morality. The ship was more like a den of furies and harpies, with men made beasts, than the resort of discipline, order, and sobriety. It was, perhaps, wisely done in one respect, for it prevented desertion, and, in those times of stirring war and active service, desertion was a calamity not easily repaired. The men were the outcasts of prisons—fellows who, in the times of our savage penal code, had just weathered the gallows, and bore up, as the next and easiest resource, for the navy. These, intermixed with the good, old, noble, generous tar, placed the sailor sometimes in a bad position. To retain this heterogeneous mixture in some degree of security, it was absolutely necessary to provide them on board with the only pleasures they sought for on shore. Hence the introduction of women, dancing, and liberty-liquor; but as for "liberty," it was only in the song—

> "For none are so free as we sons of the wave."

Tom Bowling: A Tale of the Sea. Capt. Frederick Chamier, R.N.
(London, 1841. Henry Colburn.)

———•———

The new captain of the *Echo* was well aware that he could trust many of his men on shore. It was an honour to belong to the *Echo;* and all the women (those women make a man's fame) cheered the seamen of the gallant little craft, and were all anxious to be noticed by them. Whether this arose from admiration of their bravery, or a knowledge of their probable amount of prize-money, is difficult to determine. Worldly aggrandizement, or the increased possession of wealth, is very consonant with the ideas of all. About twenty men had permission to go on shore for twenty-four hours, and before they were landed they were all mustered on deck. They were fine, hardy fellows; complexions as dark as mahogany; most undeniable tails; the front hair in curls; neck exposed; long-quartered shoes; and with enough canvas in their inexpressibles to capsize a jolly-boat. Every man's cheek seemed as if he put an apple in his mouth, the quid being a never-failing companion. They all wore stockings; but as to gloves, Jack would as soon think of dipping his feet in wooden shoes as his hands in leather.

Tom Bowling: A Tale of the Sea. Capt. Frederick Chamier, R.N.
(London, 1841. Henry Colburn.)

———•———

The ship was scarcely anchored at Spithead when she was surrounded by numerous wherries, filled with people who endeavoured to make their way on board. Jew jostled Christian, and Christian jostled Jew— all the good things the town of Portsmouth could supply changed places with pea-coffee, sea-pies, lobscouse, and salt-junk. The bumboat women, who were seated in the stern sheets of their well-appointed wherries, blocked up with legs of mutton, pounds of butter, quartern loaves, beef sausages, and casks of porter, anxiously endeavoured to obtain the preference. A bumboat woman is generally a character; and to be a genuine species of her tribe she should not weigh less than fourteen stone: the nearer she approaches to sixteen the greater her originality. She has been a fresh-coloured pretty girl, with good teeth, much chat, and more assurance, and has in her time captivated the hearts of more than one officer; this she knows well how to turn to her own advantage. The remains of beauty are still to be seen in her complexion and good-humoured face, which is generally improved by the effects of the sea breeze. Her boat is small, and her stock of goods entirely fills it. . . . It is then quite necessary that the fat fair one should first occupy her place in the boat, which naturally becomes considerably by the stern: to counterbalance this, a cask of porter is stowed away forward, to bring the boat, as it is intended to do the purchasers, by the head; then the joints of meat, loaves of bread, and other good things, are packed near their mistress, and made all snug, to be in perfect trim when the waterman has taken his seat. Thus arranged, she contrives to be on board every morning before eight o'clock, at which time the ship's company have need of her wares to assist furnishing their breakfast.

To be mistress of her art, she ought to be as perfect as Cramer or Braham in the knowledge of flats and sharps, and have a capital ear for music in the sound of a guinea; liberal when she is sure of being profitably repaid, cold as charity when that desirable end is in any way doubtful. She should have a smile like a cherubim, and an eye like a hawk, to enable her to look into the heart of the party she is about to trust, yet be able to give tick with a good grace and affability of manner, so as to make believe all reasonable doubt of you is a stranger to her soul. All these qualities will not constitute perfection unless she be well skilled in the contraband trade, and can smuggle spirits on board for the sailors, and cigars and silks on shore for the officers.

The Saucy Jack. By a Blue Jacket. (London, 1840. Richard Bentley.)

———— •●• ————

Gibraltar was the next place we proceeded to, and our passage through the "gut," as it is elegantly called, was celebrated with champagne. Hankom grew enthusiastic over his third bottle, and calling all the youngsters round him, tried to make us drunk. He succeeded in becoming so himself at all events; grew tremendously warlike, and rolled about the gun-room, vowing that he would stand by his country—which he was quite unfit to do—and was carried to his hammock peaceably.

Gibraltar is an enormous rock, the top of which is peopled by apes, and the bottom by soldiers. . . . The town is narrow, and not particularly elegant; the inhabitants ugly, and not particularly clean.

Biscuits and Grog. The personal reminiscences and sketches of Percival Plug, R.N.
(late Midshipman of H.M.S. *Preposterous*.) James Hannay.
(London, Second edition, 1848. John and D. A. Darling.)

CHAPTER IX

NAVAL DIALECT

It was a standard eighteenth century joke, repeated in a score of plays and novels, that the sailor spoke a language which no landsman could understand. The thing became traditional, and sailors willing to do what was expected of them began if anything to intensify their nautical character when ashore. Inevitably, they acted the part. The officers were not free from this tendency. Some of these, it is true, like Jane Austen's heroes, were not easily distinguishable in manner from other gentlemen; but there were others, clearly, who took pains to play the "bluff sea-dog." It is interesting to find, however, that the officers of the early nineteenth century had already developed a professional dialect distinct from that of the lower deck. Technicalities might abound, just as in the sailors' jargon, but their conversation had also a peculiar quality of its own: a dry unsmiling humour of a conventional kind which entailed the repeating of many well-worn jests at which no one was expected to laugh. This sort of humour appears in only one novel of the period—"The Post Captain"—but it is so distinctive that there can be no doubt of its having existed. It is not the sort of dialogue an author could invent. To take one or two trivial examples, we have the officer about to take the Middle Watch saying, "Damn all watches! I would sell mine to anybody for a trifle." Again, there is the question, "Where's your wife, Hurricane?"—to which the answer is, "She is in the main-top, picking gooseberries." As a final example, the following conversation will do:—

"Well, I must go below. I get no more rest than the vane at the mast-head. Taffarel! take care the ship does not fall overboard."

"Aye, aye, sir! aye, aye! But Mr. Hurricane, hark you, you have not told me which way the ship's head is?"

"Her head is between the two cat-heads."

Now, these are obviously jokes which might be repeated every week, if not every day, for a lifetime. They would be uttered and heard, one supposes, with perfect gravity. Not especially funny, even in the first instance, there is nevertheless about them a certain quality which evidently lingered on right through the nineteenth century. It is a quality which appears again, with the same mark of authenticity, in Mr. Masefield's novels "Sard Harker" and "The Bird of Dawning." Among the following pieces, the first is an

instance of this sort of conversation, taken from "The Post Captain."
The rest are in the tradition of Commodore Trunnion and merely illustrate
the sailor's cherished inability to exclude nautical technicalities from his
everyday talk, even when ashore.

"Hurricane," said the captain, "I am very glad you brought the young
lady on board. I hate to see a priest. A ship never gets safe to port that
has a priest in her; but a fine girl is a charming acquisition."

"Should the merchant and his lady, sir, incommode you, I will
willingly give up my cabin to them in the gun-room."

"I thank you kindly! Take a severe turn there! I would rather have
them in my cabin. If the wife was old and ugly, they should descend
into the gun-room; but, as she is young and pretty, I will keep them
aloft."

"Is not Flora, sir, a French name?"

"Yes it is; it is Creole French."

"But the lady, sir, is English. Her husband at least said so."

"He may tell that to the marines, but the sailors will not believe him."

"I think, sir, she is a Creole."

"You may tell it by the peak of her mizzen."

"How fine she had rigged herself, when I brought her, sir, on board."

"She was under a press of sail. She had royals set; skyscrapers, moonrakers, and a cursed god above all."

"Will it not be necessary, sir, to put down the lady as a passenger?"

"Yes."

"She has a delicate skin, sir."

"Faith! she has. She is as fair as driven charcoal."

The steward again appeared, to announce that the cold meat was laid
out in the cabin.

"Very well," said the captain. "Get some wine to pass. Come,
Hurricane, let us board the beef in the smoke."

The Post Captain, or the Wooden Walls well Manned; comprehending a view
of naval society and manners. John Davis. (First published in 1805.
Reprinted, 1928. Thomas Tegg.)

———————•◆•———————

With one spring from his cabin-door on to the gun-room table,
a vault upon deck, aided by the rim of the skylight, he hastily descended
the brig's side and jumped into the boat ere she had been completely
manned. But his flight was not unattended by defeat, for the boat had
hardly reached her destination half-way when he thought he perceived
the coxswain eyeing his dress with a significant look, as if he had detected
his borrowed plumage.

"Why, coxswain," said Burton, "you seem to be overhauling my rigging very closely—is there anything amiss?"

"I doesn't exactly know, Sir; but it looks to me, Sir, as if you'd carried away the weather topping-lift of your trowsers—the lee-leach, you see, Sir, is as slack as water."

"Curse it! if I hav'n't carried away my braces springing up that infernal skylight. Back-water your starboard oars—no, avast there—give way again—won't do to go back to the brig—I'll make shift with one o' yours."

"*Mine*, Sir!" said the coxswain, startled at the lieutenant's entertaining the idea that a sailor ever wore a suspender in his life. "*Mine*, Sir! I hope you don't take me for a soger, Sir! *I* never wants anything to keep the eyes of *my* rigging from slipping over the hounds o' the mast. But here's a bit o' rope yarn in the bottom o' the boat."

"Why, Bill," said the bowman, "there's a piece of dry parcelling in the locker abaft, as 'ill make a good preventer-brace on a pinch."

"That's right, Jones," said the lieutenant, brightening up at the bowman's suggestion. "That's right, my man—put me in mind to-morrow to give you a glass of grog for the thought."

"Aye, aye, Sir," cried Jones, with good-humoured dryness—"*I'll* freshen your memory, if *you'll* only freshen the nip."

Casting a glance once more at the flag-staff on shore, and dreading any further expenditure of powder from that quarter, he was fain to avail himself of the bowman's substitute and consult the coxswain, instead of his mirror as to his appearance. That arbiter of fashion, after examining the lieutenant as fastidiously as a boatswain would a ship, when employed in a boat ahead, squaring yards, and repeating the usual commands on such occasions.

"Top away on your starboard lift—now lower a little o' your larboard —hold-on of all—there you are, Sir,"—concluded with the consolatory assurance that all was now "square by the lifts and braces, and everything taut fore-and-aft."

Sailors and Saints; or Matrimonial Manœuvres. By the author of the "Naval Sketch Book." (London, 1829. Henry Colburn.)

———————•———————

As Lanyard got on with the dinner he cast off his reserve, and the conversation was animated although very annoying to Susan, who sat by, crimsoning at every word.

"When we came to strip her," said Lanyard, "she was very defective. The eyes of the stays were sadly worn, but she looked a better figure all bare than when she was covered with rigging. She has the neatest run fore-and-aft, from her cat-heads to her quarters, that ever I saw. From her cutwater to her stern-post there's not a nicer model; and from her head to her stern she's perfection itself."

"A little padded and bolstered under her rigging," said Bowling, chuckling at his wife's crimson cheeks, and wishing to lead Lanyard on a little: "What do you think of her qualities?"

"She's s hallow in her hold, but carries her provisions well; her berths are all good and she never labours much. She works uncommonly well, and is always quick and easy in stays."

This last was too much for Susan, and she asked, with as much forbearance as she could command, who might be the subject of such very free conversation.

"You shall see her to-morrow," said Bowling.

"You never saw a greater beauty in your life, ma'am," said Lanyard. "I'll take care she's well stoned and scrubbed, and you shall see her as neat and as clean as any quality lady in the land. If we were not in Portsmouth harbour, we might dress her out a little; those colours always set her off. The gig is all ready and the whip's easily prepared."

"I must insist upon knowing," said Susan, "who this lady is, of whom you both speak so familiarly."

"Lady!" said Lanyard, with his eyes staring as if he thought Mrs. Bowling was mad. "Lady, Ma'am! Why, we are talking of the ship and her boat—the *Thames* and her gig."

Tom Bowling: A Tale of the Sea. Capt. Frederick Chamier, R.N. (London, 1841. Henry Colburn.)

———————•—•———————

A fine morning, and a slight respite from pain, at length enabled the veteran to appear in the well-walk to make his observations on the place and company in person. Being unable to walk he came in that sort of conveyance, so common at Cheltenham, a wheeled-chair, which was drawn or rather propelled by Tiller "abaft," whilst the invalid, with a good-humoured smile at the singularity of the conveyance, took the helm in hand and steered himself according to Thomas's pilotage.

Tiller, who was expert at "conning" craft of every description, and who directed the course of the veteran's chair, afforded to many considerable amusement by his technical language and singular deportment.

"Mind your port-helm," said he, "Keep the steeple open with the trees—there we are, Sir—right in mid-channel—steady—e—a—starboard with all, Sir."

"Starboard it is," echoed the commodore.

"Starboard *yet*, i' you please, Sir."

108

"What, still? why—she gripes most confoundedly, Thomas!"

One or two of those nice bilious and interesting looking gentlemen, who had taken their "*second* tumbler," and already experienced some squeamishness in the abdominal region, seemed suddenly "taken aback," as if they sympathized with this nautical allusion and were perceived as suddenly "altering their course."

"Gripes *very* much indeed," repeated the veteran.

"Well, Sir," said Tiller, "we must only brail up abaft. But if we gripe now, what 'ill it be byne bye when we come to take in our water!"

"Why, yes, Thomas, we musn't bring her too much by the head."

"I know it brought many *there* oftener than they wished t'ether morning."

Notwithstanding the anxiety Crank had expressed, to betake himself to the use of the waters as speedily as possible, he made the circuit of Mother Forty's Well without "shortening sail"; and even coasted all round the adjoining pump-room without coming once to an anchor.

Sailors and Saints, or Matrimonial Manoeuvres. By the author of the "Naval Sketch Book." (London, 1829. Henry Colburn.)

PRIZE-MONEY

Prize-money played a larger part in the naval life of Nelson's day than later historians are willing to admit. There were large fortunes to be made in the navy—fortunes perhaps larger and more numerous than were to be made in any other profession—made more rapidly than in any other trade. In the generation of the French Wars several admirals became what we should now call millionaires. They seem sometimes to have been regarded as the 'nouveaux riches' of the day, as the nabobs had been a generation earlier. Captains, even, had been known to make respectable fortunes. It is not therefore to be wondered at if naval officers welcomed the outbreak of war and then intrigued to be stationed in a profitable quarter of the globe. These "expert and speculative" frigate captains could often found a county family on the proceeds of their campaigns.

Like their officers, the seamen—especially those in cruisers and frigates— lived in hope of prize-money. Their share seldom amounted to any great sum, but they sometimes received it rather more promptly than they received their pay. The tradition was for them to spend all their money almost as soon as they came ashore. The last piece quoted below shows how they could spend their prize-money before it was even paid to them. The officers had a similar system of a more genteel kind. They received "advances" from their agents.

According to the practice of the period, some of our more expert and speculative cruisers, particularly commanders of fast-sailing frigates, entered into mutual compact to share in the profits of all prizes captured apart. They appointed a specified latitude and longitude for rendezvous, and agreed to communicate the result of their respective success. Such a compact was formed between Captain T. and Captain P. Six weeks often would elapse, ere, with crowded canvas, the cruisers discovered each other. On one occasion, communicating by signal, the ship of Captain P., a long way to leeward, asked if Captain T. "had taken any-thing?" The answer was "Yes." The number representing this word remained flying so long that the first interrogator, losing all patience,

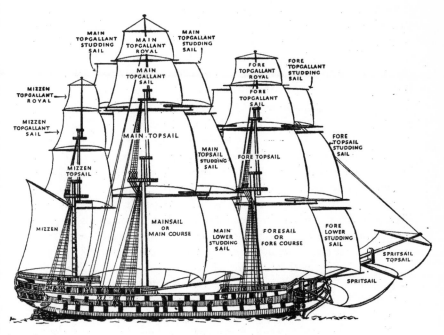

MAIN
TOPGALLANT
STUDDING
SAIL

MAIN
TOPGALLANT
ROYAL

MAIN
TOPGALLANT
STUDDING
SAIL

FORE
TOPGALLANT
ROYAL

FORE
TOPGALLANT
STUDDING
SAIL

MIZZEN
TOPGALLANT
ROYAL

MAIN
TOPGALLANT
SAIL

FORE
TOPGALLANT
SAIL

MIZZEN
TOPGALLANT
SAIL

MAIN TOPSAIL

FORE
TOPSAIL
STUDDING
SAIL

MIZZEN
TOPSAIL

MAIN
TOPSAIL
STUDDING
SAIL

FORE TOPSAIL

MIZZEN

MAINSAIL
OR
MAIN COURSE

MAIN
LOWER
STUDDING
SAIL

FORESAIL
OR
FORE COURSE

FORE
LOWER
STUDDING
SAIL

SPRITSAIL
TOPSAIL

SPRITSAIL

PLATE 11—Sail-plan of a 74-gun ship.

111

and stimulated by the expectation of gain, demanded "What?" "Physic," replied T—.

Naval Sketch Book, or the Service Afloat and Ashore. (Second series. London, 1834. Whittaker and Co.)

———·●·———

We were cruising off the coast of Italy and had been very unsuccessful in the way of captures; our martial ardour, or empty pockets, had called into existence the desire of glory or gain. No doubt glory is a very fine thing but honour will not mend a broken leg, whereas gain will pay the apothecary's bill. I merely mention this, because we hear a great deal about honour and glory, and such like, and no one is candid enough to say that lucre—vile, filthy lucre, has anything to do with the business; but we "sea attorneys" know better. I have known the prize-money shared in imagination, previous to the capture, and honour and glory never mentioned in the calculation.

The Life of a Sailor. By a Captain in the Navy. (London, 1832. Richard Bentley.)

———·●·———

As I was taking notes of these ideas at the *George*, where I was engaged to dine yesterday with some naval friends, a very young officer but very old seaman, made his *entrée*, vociferating, "Thank my stars, we are likely to have a war of some length!" "What," said his associate, "you would not surely wish to sacrifice the lives of thousands to your own private interest? That would be to reverse the moral axiom, that the good of the individual should ever give way to the good of the whole."

"Avast hauling on that thought, shipmate, it's fathom and half too deep for me! I'm above board, d'ye see! and if I am to be in commission, I like to have something to do; I likes to be in an action, and would be rather blowing a match at any time than blowing my fingers! There's life in that! but as to a dead peace, d'ye see, there's nothing to me so vexatious, except it be a dead calm. At such times everything is flat; even our newspapers not having a paragraph fit to meet the eye of a seaman. Landlord, let us have a glass of grog, such as *seamen* might be thought to relish. So, that's the sort. But as to *war*, there's sound and sense in that word! It's like a brisk gale, the main-spring of motion: then, indeed, you'll hear of a battle! Bore down upon a wind, open our lower-deckers, tip them a *Jaculator*, engage yardarm and yardarm, run up the sides like lamp-lighters, carve our way sword in hand to the quarter-deck, deal about death at every blow: she strikes! That's life! Take her in tow! share the corianders, and spend them at the George, half and half; that's life! What says *Cox*, eh, old boy?"

"Oh, Sir, we publicans must ever submit to sentiments like these; 'there's life in them.'" "That there is, my honest fellow! Tip us your daddle for that." Saying which, he turned round *upon a heel*, singing, as he rocked along, "Oh, what a charming thing's a *battle!*"

The Naval Guardian. By Charles Fletcher, M.D.
(Second edition. London, 1805. For various publishers, including Longman, Hurst, Rees, and Orme, of Paternoster Row, and P. Steel of Tower Hill.)

NOTE: A "jaculator"—A fish, whose chief sustenance is flies, and its mode of securing which seems truly singular: It is by shooting a single drop of water from its mouth upon the insect, which never fails to kill it, and that at a considerable distance.

So I left Betsy, who was a cloth or two in the wind and sailing a little by the head, with the rest; and away I steered to Moses. He was at home, or some one so cursedly like him, that I should not have known one from the other; but all Jews are alike. The shark knew me, for many's the time I had taken a jacket from his kit when he came on board, and knowing how sharp these fellows are to catch a seaman I thought I would let him bite at the bait well before I hooked him; so said I, "Moses, here we are, all alive, and with plenty of prizes"—To be sure that was rather more smoke than reality.

"My Gosh! yes," says Moses, "how much wosh you take for your prize-money?"

"There's a nibble! thought I, this fellow would swallow bait, hook, line, and all.—"How much, Moses? Why, how much do you think I ought to get?"

"Five pounds," says Moses.

"Five devils!" says I; "more like fifty, and that would hardly be enough for all the work we have had."

"It's a sight of money, Mr. Toprail," said Moses, "fifty pounds! it vill be long times before it is paid, ay?"

"Yes," said I, "so long that a man might die before he got it. What's the price of this new turn-out here?".

"Oh, it's very sheap, Mr. Toprail, very sheap, just three pounds, only one little three pounds. You can take it, Mr. Toprail, upon the security of your prize money. If you make me your agent, I can let you have many things: as you say, you may be dead and buried before the money is paid. Come, I'll give you twenty pounds and this suit of clothes for your share. You are an A.B., I know."

"Then you know wrong, my jolly friend Moses, for I'm captain of the fore-top."

"Petty officer's rating," said Moses. "Fifty pounds! quite impossible. I'll give you thirty—thirty now, this morning, in one hour, and that's more worth to you, Mr. Toprail, than fifty, four years from this time."

"Thirty, and the suit of rigging complete: white ducks, blue jacket, black tie, white stockings, long-quartered shoes, new hat with Royal Sovereign marked on the ribbon. That, or go. Give us your hand upon it. I dare say you will get more than half back in traps. . . ."

Ben Brace, the last of Nelson's Agamemnons. Captain Frederick Chamier, R.N. (London, 1836. Richard Bentley.)

CHAPTER XI

RELIGION

The official religion upheld in a man-of-war was that of the Church of England. Ships of the line often carried chaplains, and in other vessels it was not unusual for the captain or purser to read the service on Sunday, now and again, if it happened to be fine. Such services were often perfunctory enough, as may well be supposed, but it would be a mistake to suppose that this was invariable. Many captains were extremely religious in a formal way, and their officers no less so. It is doubtful, however, whether this kind of religion had much hold on the seamen. At any rate, the navy seems to have offered a fine opportunity to the methodist preachers. It was no uncommon thing to hear of prayer-meetings being held on the lower deck. Although normally disapproving, the officers could find nothing in the Articles of War about hymn singing, and so felt unable to interfere. The movement would not have spread so widely as it did, perhaps, had it not been for the conversion of one or two captains and the enthusiastic support of Lord Gambier. Under this methodist admiral a sound evangelical theology became a sure, and perhaps even the only, road to promotion, or so it was believed. In the first of the following pieces, it is presumably Lord Gambier who is portrayed as "Sir Jemmy the Good." Although apparently harmless, methodism, if sufficiently widespread in a ship, could undermine discipline and occasionally did so.

The tracts, passages from which conclude this chapter, are by an ex-naval lieutenant who became a preacher at Penzance. They date from a rather later period but may be taken as fairly representing the spirit of the movement and the obstacles to its progress that existed in the minds and habits of the seamen.

Amongst the other duties, which Fitzjohn had assigned to him, was that of telling old Mac when the commander-in-chief showed his nose, and when he hid the same, as the following example will show.

Whilst double-reefing the main-topsail one day, the commander-in-chief being below, old Mac was calling out to the men aloft, in that most energetic, but I must add ungentleman-like style, at that time common in the navy, "You d——d infernal scoundrels, will you bear a-hand or must I cut the rascally livers out of every one of you? You blackguards! if that sail isn't well reefed in two minutes and a half—I'll——." Here Fritz, seeing Sir Jemmy the Good make his appearance, pulled old Mac by the sleeve and whispered, "Admiral is on deck, sir."

Powers of civility! what a change came over Mac's dream! The rigid muscles which anger had so lately called into full play smoothed away like the quick subsiding foam of spirit, nor did his language become less altered. "Come, my good fellows," said Old Mac, "be quick and reef the main-topsail, do now; but don't hurry in from the yardarms, lest any of you fall overboard." Here the commander-in-chief, thinking that there was more wind blowing than would do him good, dived below once more.

"Admiral gone below, sir," said Fitzjohn, ever watchful. No sooner did old Mac hear the joyful news than he burst forth with his peculiar eloquence once more.

"O you d—— scowbanking lubbers, why the devil don't you move your lazy limbs! May I never move hand or foot again if I don't flog the last man in from each yardarm!" And such, or similar to this, was the pantomime almost daily acted on board the *Puritan*, in fifty different ways. Mac was to have a frigate, if himself and the admiral jogged on well, and though he had serious faults—impediments of speech, as it were—still poor Mac richly deserved his ship from his long and faithful services.

Gentleman Jack, A Naval Story. W. Johnson Neale. (London, 1837. Henry Colburn.)

———————•———————

"Apropos of old women, I went on board that fine three-decker, the *None-such*, the other day, gentlemen," said Lackwit (who now thought as he grew warmed with wine and grog the time was come to bear a part in the conversation), "and you never saw such a mess as she was in, I don't mean her decks, but on the quarter-deck were unpacking two or three bales of Bibles, and serving out to the ship's company—while the first lieutenant investigated (under the captain's occasional higher superintendence) the peculiar qualities of each candidate—the skipper, such a figure I never before saw in my life!" "How do you mean, Mr. Lackwit," asked Weazel—"Why sir, I mean in *dress!*—he was walking up and down the larboard side with his hands in his pockets, dressed more like an old clothes man than the captain of a three-decker." "Why, how *was* he dressed? I've heard as he's turned *psalm singer*," said Weazel. "Why, sir," continued Lackwit, "he had on an old surtout coat, turned quite green, patched with new blue cloth, and some places sewn up with white thread!—and neither straps nor epaulettes on, an old beaver turned up behind—sat on the nape of his neck, almost falling off his head—with a pair of greasy blue stocking pantaloons on, and coarse worsted grey stockings, and his shoes like a ploughman's!" "Truly a very pretty figure," said Classic, "but what did he say?" "Why, sir, at first I could not believe it was the captain, till I heard him *sing out*, as I went over to where he was walking, to speak to an old messmate of mine; he called out to the first lieutenant, who seemed busy enough, handing out the Bibles—

"Mr. —— a—a—a—see—see that they understand the nature of it—and—a—a—make no dog ears—and take great care of it, and put it by in their chests carefully—and mind they read it often—those who you find, d——n me, anyway backward, let them be put in a class, to commune with those good men, Tom Hopeful and James Holystone on the forecastle—and d'ye hear, Mr. —— a—a—a—, let it be known that I'll have no swearing, d——n me! no swearing! I shall take notice of those that behave properly and meekly, and subdue all unruly passions and wickedness! Any that are rampant and wicked, and use profane words, I'll put in the black list as sure as they live, d——n me—and flog, d——n me!"

The Navy at Home. (London, 1831. William Marsh.)

———————•❦•———————

". . . I remember, one day, as I was taking a caulk on my chest in the berth, who should come forward, you know, but the captain's cox'n. 'Well,' says he, 'rise, my man, 'tis time afore this you'd a *call*.' 'Why d——n it,' says I, 'it's my watch below!' 'Watch below!' says he, turning up his eyes like a lady in love, 'ah, Sam! 'tis time you should think of your watch above.' Well, I'm blow'd if I knew what the fellow was at, so I let him go on for awhile. When, 'Sam,' says he, looking me straight in the face, 'you're sure to be damn'd for your sins.' 'The devil I am; who told you?' says I. 'I tells you,' says he, 'unless you gets—(let's see, what was the word) unless you gets—you gets—I have him—you gets—Re—Re—jenny—*rated*,' says he. 'What ship's that? get *rated what?*' says I. 'Born'd all over again,' says he. 'What, tarn a fellow into *Twicelaid?*' says I. 'Aye, and tarn from your sins,' says he. So, to shorten the matter, says I, 'I tell you what it is, Mr. Cox'n, every man to his station'—'the cook to the fore-sheet'; you may be a very good hand at the helm—but a precious poor pilot for heaven. You're out of your latitude now; keep within soundings,' says I, 'and talk like a sensible man; when it's comfort I wants, 'tis not to the likes of such fellows as you that I'll seek; I'll look to the *log-book aloft*; so brace up and haul aft and no more of your preaching,' says I. Well, I silenced his fire, for he never came near me again."

The Naval Sketch Book. By an Officer of Rank.
(Second edition. London, 1826. Henry Colburn.)

───────●───────

PLYMOUTH DOCK

(Sailors meeting in the street).

Bob: Yo ho, shipmate, what ship?

James: I belong, my brother, to the *Royal George,* in Cawsand Bay.

Bob: You've slipt your cable and run on shore then, my boy.

James: I landed two days since, and am going on board, according to orders, to-morrow.

Bob: Fine weather on shore, shipmate; plenty of pirates in the harbour, dashing away with prize-money: saw two pendants flying this morning—made sail—they stood off—gave chase—they tacked and stood across the street—I luffed up, lay right in the wind's eye—they bore away—squared my yards—out studding sails—sung out, steady—ranged up alongside on their starboard quarter—poured in a broadside—they struck—took them in tow, and saw them moored about an hour since close aboard the rocks. What say, shipmate, wilt share the prizes?

James: Thank ye, shipmate, but I'd rather be excused; you are very frank in communicating the particulars of your cruise, but it would have afforded me far more pleasure to have heard a better account of the manner in which you have spent your time on shore.

Bob: Time, shipmate! time on shore! What's time for—but that a fellow may enjoy himself while he has it, especially on shore? Why, I wouldn't give a rope's end for that man who doesn't make hay while the sun shines, as long as his liberty ticket lasts.

James: If you mean that we should improve the time allowed us by our officers to be on shore, so that we may be gratified with the reflection of it on board, you have my hearty concurrence; but if you mean that we should rush into all the vices that we possibly can on shore, because we must soon go on board again, I hope you will not be angry with me if I differ from you on that point.

Bob: Angry! Why, no, shipmate, I'm not angry, d'ye see, but you seem to be a vessel under false colours. I'm upright and downright, and, if so be you'll bear away with me to Rotten Row, why, about ship—and if not, sheer off—or (here a dreadful volley of oaths succeed).

James: I'm truly sorry, my brother, than any observation of mine should induce you to swear so awfully . . . and I cannot express the grief I feel that you appear so insensible to your immortal interests as to plunge body and soul into hell, for the momentary gratification of the basest lusts. (Tears of pity trickle down the manly cheeks of James.)

Bob: Avast there—avast there, messmate—clap a stopper on that there rope: come, come, no broadside yet—you've no leak in the hull—let's have none of the eye-pumps at work—why you make me think of the time when Poll piped her eye all the way on shore, because we were ordered out to the Indies. Stand fast, messmate, you seem to be a good fellow—let's make sail for the Nelson, at North Corner, and take in a double allowance of grog.

James: It pains my mind, shipmate, to be obliged to reject this request also; because I know it flows from an abundance of good nature in you; but indeed, my brother, I've no taste for any company or accommodation to be had at a public-house in a seaport town. There was a time—O my God, that I am yet spared!

Bob: Ha! ha! brother, what, you are there, are you? I thought we should soon find out what sort of stuff you're made of. What, you are a methodist lubber, are you? What, preach to a fellow in the open street? Why, split my jib-boom if I wouldn't sooner be a loblolly boy, or a Frenchman, than a methodist—all hands, up anchor a-hoy—tumble up there—tumble up there, my boys. Shipmate, I shall up skyscrapers and moonrakers, so don't give chase.

The Boatswain's Mate, or an interesting dialogue between two British Seamen. Rev. G. C. Smith, formerly of the Navy. (London, n.d. W. Whittemore. The Repository for Religious Tracts, Sunday School Books, etc.)

THE THEATRE

James: I remember some years back being on shore in London with several shipmates one Saturday; after rolling about the streets and drinking excessively, we rushed into the Royal Circus, in Blackfriars Road, and entered the gallery while the actors were performing. The house was crowded; I proposed that we should fight our way with the sticks we had, to the front of the gallery, and each of us leap from thence into the pit: this was resolved on, with dreadful imprecations on the man that failed. I sallied forth, leading the van, and desperately encountering everyone that opposed us. After many struggles with the audience, I reached the front of the gallery, and sung out to the people below, "Stand from under, there." Several gentlemen interposed to prevent me, but I fought with a large stick like a madman, and calling to my shipmates, "Are you all ready? here goes." I leaped off—when (O my God, why was I spared from the bottomless pit?) a gentleman caught me by the greatcoat, and hung me there until others could drag me in. The theatre was all confusion—the acting was stopped—and the runners dragged my shipmates downstairs in the most brutal manner. A police officer seized me—a scuffle ensued—I struck him with such violence as to endanger his life. I endeavoured to escape, but a blow from another officer across my arm rendered it useless and they overpowered me. I attempted to raise a mob to rescue me, but the officer forced us into a coach and hurried us into St. George's watch-house in the borough. There we roared and sang the most infamous songs until three o'clock on the Sabbath morning, when we fell asleep. At seven o'clock we were roused by the people in the street calling to us and pitying us as poor harmless sailors, who only happened to be drunk; we told a piteous tale and they brought us liquor until we were almost intoxicated again! I strove to be merry, but my conscience stung me to that degree that I shook with horror at my situation. My companions knew nothing and cared for nothing, but I had received a religious education: I had been trained up at Surrey Chapel Sunday School. . . .

The Quartermaster, or the Second Part of the Boatswain's Mate. Being an interesting dialogue between two British seamen. (New edition. London, n.d. D. Cox, Southwark.)

------------◆------------

THE MESSMATES

Several of the crew had already made Bob a subject of conversation; but the general concerns of the ship having required the attention of every man, they had no leisure to say much: the ship was, however, now placed on the sea establishment. Bob messed in the starboard bay, and, with the exception of the gunner's yeoman, all his shipmates were desperately wicked men. Pat Flannagan was a wild Irishman; Jack Capstan was a Gosport waterman; Dick Mainmast was a native of Wapping; Harry Windlass had been a Cornish fisherman in Mounts Bay; Francois, or Fransa as they called him, was from Paris: he was taken in a boat and entered into the English service; Sambo was a free black from Antigua; Donald, the gunner's yeoman, was from Aberdeen: his education had been the means of restraining him from the vices around him, and though an unregenerate man, yet he often checked his messmates for their language and conduct, but, as he sometimes was intoxicated with them, and occasionally, when irritated, would swear, they considered him partly in league with themselves, and therefore only laughed at his occasional reproofs. The cook for the day had just cleared the chest lid (on which they dined) of a bowl of peasoup, and brought their allowance of grog down, when they determined to attack Bob on his new religion, as they termed it. . . .

The Dreadnought, or the Fifth Part of the Boatswain's Mate. Being a continuation of interesting dialogues between British Seamen of his Majesty's Navy. By a Naval Officer. (London, n.d. D. Cox, Southwark.)

CHAPTER XII

ANECDOTES

NOTES FOR NAVAL MAXIMS
(Found in the Pocket-book of a Post Captain).

In Parliament.—On nautical topics observe a passive and dignified silence. The discussion of naval affairs and maritime matters to be left solely to landsmen.

In command.—Should you be a flag-officer, neglect not to favour the fleet with a ceaseless succession of signals, monotonous movements, new circulars, and old orders. In the concoction of official papers, verbose ambiguity to be studiously sought.

Naval Sketch Book, or the Service Afloat and Ashore. (Second series. London, 1834. Whittaker and Co.)

———————•❧•———————

This man had just been paid off from a large frigate, commanded by some Tartar, who made no scruple of sending for his warrant-officers at all hours of the night. This slavery, therefore, was past, and, having done with superior officers for the present, our boatswain might sleep the night out in security. But this was not sufficient for this moral epicure, and, to enjoy the luxury to the utmost, he gave orders to his boy to come and shake him by the shoulder every morning at one o'clock, saying, "Sir, the captain wants you on the forecastle immediately." Accordingly the boy called him, as he desired, when he gruffly growled out:

"Holloa! holloa! what's the matter now?"

"Captain wants you, sir, on the deck directly."

"Are you sure he wants me?"

"Oh, yes, sir, wants you very bad indeed."

"Is there a h——l of a rout up there?"

"Yes, sir, a terrible fuss, surely: there's the fore-yard gone in the slings; the gammoning of the bowsprit stranded; one of the cat-heads carried away, and the starboard bow-port stove in."

"Then you're positive he's hard up for want of me?"

"Yes, sir, sure."

"Then d—— his eyes, boy, tell him I won't come!"

Cavendish; or the Patrician at Sea. (Second edition. London, 1832. Henry Colburn and Richard Bentley.)

Determined to enjoy to the fullest extent the several privileges peculiar to Parliamentary men, Sir Montague, when the "House was sitting," was sure to be the first, and often the last, seen in his political place . . . for hours and hours . . . did the gallant legislator enjoy his constitutional somnolency on the ministerial side of the back benches of St. Stephen's. Not that, when awake, Sir Montague was aught of a listener; seldom was he cognisant of the business in debate, and invariably, upon the discussion of professional topics, were his lips hermetically sealed. Indeed, upon maritime matters, he was wont to manifest a talent for taciturnity seldom surpassed by senatorial tars.

Never during a parliamentary career of six years had his sweet voice been heard in the Senate, save on one occasion, when he started from a troubled dream, and vociferated "question! question!"—though, in fact, no question happened to be before the House; and yet, when afloat, and disposed to be communicative, the Baronet's "Table-talk" seldom diverged into any other topic than that of his "contemplated motion." So constantly, indeed, was this made the theme of conversation at dinner, that in the cockpit it went by no other name than the "Skipper's *perpetual motion.*"

Land Sharks and Sea Gulls. Captain Glascock, R.N.
(London, 1838. Richard Bentley.)

———————•———————

It is within the memory of man that a duel was fought at Calcutta between two midshipmen—the cause of the quarrel I forget, that is quite immaterial—a quarrel they had, and a duel was the consequence. On this occasion the gunner and boatswain were the two seconds. As neither party had seen a duel before, and consequently had no more idea of the law on this subject than an Esquimaux has of comfort, they imagined that they were to take an active part in the concern and re-paired with their principals to an appointed spot. The ground was measured at eighteen paces, when the gunner, who had often seen a prize-fight and imagined a second was to behave in the present affair the same as in a boxing-match, knelt upon one knee, and placed his man thereupon, saying aloud: "Now then, Yarn, my man's ready; why don't you set your backstay up?" Yarn called out, "that there was something the matter with the lanyard of the pistol (meaning the trigger), for that he had been endeavouring to scale the guns for half an hour, and his man swore he would have a match in preference." This delayed the affair. The gunner, however, easing the lock by means of a knife, the parties took up their places on their seconds' knees, and there loaded the pistols. Although the enmity was great on the part of the principals, the seconds had always been, until now, good friends, and when both had answered, "All ready on this side," they each began to edge nearer to their adversaries, the seconds supporting the arm of the principal, and giving wholesome advice. "We are quite out of range," said Priming, the gunner, "let's get close on board him before we fire." In the meantime, Yarn was recommending the first broadside, and, as his principal was damning the lock because it went too hard, Yarn got his forefinger to bear upon the trigger, and stood by for a haul. At this moment, Priming's man's pistol went off, the ball passing through the rim of Yarn's hat. "That whizzed over my top-lights; now, sir, blaze away!" whereupon they both hauled at the trigger, which, of course, lowered the muzzle of the pistol: off it went, and the ball, instead of knocking out some of the head-rails of the enemy, struck his foot and left him lame for life. The gunner swore "he would not strike his colours," but the pain was so great that his principal fainted before Yarn and his man could get another shot ready; they were so occupied loading the pistol that they never remarked that their fire had taken effect. "Bear a hand," says Yarn, "mind the cartridge, stern foremost, and seam downwards, I'll ram him home—there now—handle the lanyard and blaze away." At this moment Priming hailed that "his man had struck his colours," upon which Yarn roared out, "Hurrah! now, sir, knock Priming's other eye out (he had but one), and then we'll take possession of the *prizes*." The enmity of Yarn's man died with the knowledge of the mischief he had done; in vain his second endeavoured to hold him on his knee, as he kept edging up to the enemy, whose fire he swore he had silenced; he recommended his principal to "fire another broadside and board him in the smoke." But Priming took the liberty of striking his colours in reality; he shouldered his wounded principal, and walked off with him to a log of wood in the vicinity. Here the business was accommodated, and the parties separated. . . .

Footnote: One of the principals I met a few days back in Paris; the wounded officer is now a lieutenant, but will be lame to his last moment.

The Life of a Sailor. By a Captain in the Navy. (London, 1832. Richard Bentley.)

———————•♦•———————

They quarrelled about rum and religion—two things often mixed together with a methodist—after having expended about as decent a set of words as could be selected from Grose's Slang Dictionary, the gunner said the boatswain was "*no* gentleman." There was no standing this insult. Mr. Pipes had, it is true, been all his life before the mast, and had associated with the very best society at either North Corner or the

Point; but he was an officer by virtue of his warrant, and that warrant made him likewise a gentleman. Pounce, the gunner, was a quiet systematic man, and proceeded to the first lieutenant, from whom he got permission for himself and the boatswain to spend the next day on shore; he then sent his compliments to Mr. Pipes, and with his words he sent a ship's musket, and a ballast-basket full of musket-ball cartridges, selecting the ground in the vicinity of St. Antonio Gardens as the rendezvous the next morning at sunrise. Before sunrise Pipes and his boy landed in a Maltese boat, and betook themselves, muskets, ballast-baskets, and cartouche-boxes, to the appointed place; and having loaded the musket, Pipes and Co. came to an anchor on a wall which separated two fields—for in Malta hedges are almost, if not entirely, unknown. At day-dawn the boatswain saw Mr. Pounce advancing with hasty strides to the spot, he being, at the time he was discovered, about half a mile distant; Pipes immediately called out—"The enemy's hove in sight!" and, to use his own expression, he "fired a shot across his bows to make him heave-to." Pounce, finding the enemy had taken up a disadvantageous situation, having his back to a wall (a circumstance which has proved fatal to more than one unfortunate fellow), desired his boy, who acted as his second, to "come to an anchor and open the magazine"; he at the same time commencing action and blazing away at Pipes. Which of the two fired the best has not been discovered, for no trace was left of ravages committed: from which it was inferred that the balls must have lodged some half mile beyond the foe. It is with great satisfaction I mention the gallant behaviour of the seconds: while the masters were loading they got ready other cartridges, bit the ends off, and looked along the barrels, indicating their approval of the aim taken, or hinting, "I think, sir, you're pointing too much aloft; why, it will go over his masthead vane"; and when both bent forward to see if the shot took effect it was invariably followed with, "I'll spoil his figurehead yet," or "I'm blowed if I did not hull him." In a very short time the powder was expended on both sides, the magazines were emptied, and the gunner came to the charge; he however soon discovered he had omitted to bring a bayonet, whereupon he sent his faithful squire with a flag of truce on a ramrod, which being favourably received by Pipes and his squire, the former advanced and said, "Master says as how, Sir, he's werry sorry he forgot the baggonet—and if so be that you've had enough for the present, he thinks as how you had better make a board for the Rosolio shop, whilst he sends off for the cheese-toasters; and, if so be you are contented with this, you're to make a signal." Upon which, the boatswain applied his whistle to his mouth, and "piped Belay," finishing with the sound, implying "let go," upon which both parties put on their peace-establishment looks, and retired in good order to breakfast, over which it was understood Mr. Pounce retracted the offensive expression. . . .

The Life of a Sailor. By a Captain in the Navy.
(London, 1832. Richard Bentley.)

————— ◆ —————

The professional reader is aware that the form which the Navy Board (now no longer extant) used, in the prodigality of its tenderness, to assume, when addressing an officer was, "we are, Sir, your *Affectionate friends*." Our worthy Sir J., who had often perceived this, thought that so much graciousness should be reciprocated, if only on the old principle, that one good turn deserves another. In this conviction, he one day subscribed himself in language similar to that which preceded the signature of the Right Honourable Commissioners. This was, at head-quarters, held to be too familiar, and a written remonstrance was conveyed to Sir J. informing him that it was unusual (to say the least of it) for officers to use such freedom with the dignity of "Boards." Sir J. took the rebuke with great composure, and acknowledged it something in the following way:—

"Gentlemen,—I have the honor to receive your letter of the ——— acquainting me that it is not according to the rules of the service for officers to subscribe themselves in the words adopted in my last. I shall be careful to obey the intimation, and meanwhile have the honor to remain,

> Gentlemen,
> *Not* your affectionate friend,
> J. P."

Naval Sketch Book, or the Service Afloat and Ashore. (Second series. London, 1834. Whittaker and Co.)

————— ◆ —————

A captain of a man-of-war, newly appointed to a ship on the Irish station, took the precaution in "beating out" of the harbour, to apprise the pilot that he was totally unacquainted with the coast, and therefore he must rely entirely on the pilot's local knowledge for the safety of the ship.

"You are perfectly sure, pilot," said the captain, "you are well acquainted with the coast?"

"Do I know my own name, Sir?"

"Well, mind, I warn you not to approach too near the shore."

"Now, make yoursel' *asy*, Sir: in troth you may go to bed if you plase."

"Then shall we stand on?"

"Why—what else wou'd we do?"

"Yes, but there *may* be hidden dangers which you know nothing about."

"Dangers? I like to see dangers *dar* hide themselves from Mick. Sure, don't I tell you I know every rock on the coast?" (here the ship strikes)—"and that's one of 'em!"

Naval Sketch Book, or the Service Afloat and Ashore. (Second series. London, 1834. Whittaker and Co.)

———————

A late most worthy admiral, who then commanded a line-of-battle-ship, mast-headed an Irish youngster, a protégé of his own, for some idleness or stupidity in his day's work. The ship was at sea, and many hundreds of miles from the nearest shore; but either with a reference to what he had been doing, or with a view of keeping him on the alert—perhaps both—he was ordered to look out for the land.

At length, the term of his punishment having expired, the captain came on deck: "Masthead there—come down, Mr. ——." The delinquent arrived on the quarter-deck, touching his hat, looking half sulky, half frightened, and very cold. "Well, Sir"—gruffly and authoritatively—"Do you see the land?" "No, Sir," answered poor Paddy, whining, "*but I can almost.*" It is needless to add that he was not sent back again.

The Naval Sketch Book. By an Officer of Rank.
(Second edition. London, 1826. Henry Colburn.)

———————

He [a midshipman] was learning mathematics, and had one day been kept by his master some time after the dinner-hour, for which the youngster wished him and his problems snug in "Davy's locker." The master was called away for a time, leaving directions for the mid to finish the problem he was about by his return, but instead of doing this, he commenced making one for himself. Upon the master's rather unexpected entry, he found the young gentleman thus occupied, and immediately seized the paper upon which he had been working. It was headed, "An easy and pleasant mode of squaring the circle!" The diagram was four people sitting at a table with a large dish before them, containing a circular joint, which they were resolutely attacking—one of the corners being embellished by the rude figure of a mustard-pot. The proof was thus given: "A,C,D,F, four friends sitting at a dinner-table; B, a round of beef; Q, the mustard-pot. A,C,D,F, having each

127

taken a little from Q, apply their knives perpendicularly to B, when, if they don't square the circle, they know nothing about mathematics, or are not so hungry as I am."

Service Afloat: comprising the personal narrative of a Naval Officer employed during the late war. (London, 1833. Richard Bentley.)

————•◦•————

"Those were times, sir," said the captain of the forecastle, "but I hope the story ain't over."

"No," answered Mr. Swallowtail, "not by no means, for shortly after this action, the *Blanche* ran ashore, and knocked her rudder off, and there she lay, of no use whatsomdever. The rudder chains were both carried away, and down it went in seven fathoms water, and we could see it, supine like, at the bottom. What was to be done in this here case? Why, nobody could tell; so the Captain he called for me. "Peter," says he, "my smart fellow"—that's what he always called me when he wanted anything, and the Captain was both a scholar and a gentleman—"Peter," says he, "what is to be done under these melancholy circumstances?" "Leave that to me, Sir," says I, "and you shall see." The Captain, my lads, as I said before, was a fine fellow, and I would have gone through fire, as well as water, to have served him and the old ship. Well, so I called to my messmate, Tom Ringbolt, a fellow who could swim like a swordfish, and says I, "Tom, follow me down to the bottom." So taking the end of a hawser in my fist, overboard we went, and passed the hawser through the mortise hole of the rudder; and then says I to Tom, "Have you got a hank of spun-yarn in your pocket, to seize the end back?" A hawser is but a tender thing, you know. "No, Peter, I ain't got any," says Tom. "Then," says I, "go up and bring one down, and I'll wait here till you come back, but don't keep me here all day." So Tom he went and brought the spun-yarn: we clapped on the seizing, came to the top of the water, and got on board."

"What!" exclaimed the uninitiated landsman who was making his first voyage to sea, "did you talk all the while you were under water, Mr. Swallowtail? How could that be?"

"To be sure we did!" replied the boatswain. "Do you think everybody is such a lubberly do-little son of a sea cook as yourself——?"

The Indiaman. By a Blue Jacket. (London, 1840. Richard Bentley.)

————•◦•————

"Talking of birthdays," resumed Winstanley, "we had a notorious fellow on board the *Hippopotamus*, when I was in his Majesty's service ——."

"Curse the *Hippopotamus*, are you going to give us another long yarn about her?" growled his messmate.

The other did not notice, but said, "This man was an incorrigible drunkard, and could not be kept from intoxication. Flogging and every species of punishment had been tried in vain. He was brought aft upon the old charge, and was at the time scarcely able to stand upon his legs. "How comes it, you scoundrel, that I again see you in this disgraceful situation?" demanded the officer.

"Please, Sir, it is my birthday," answered the sailor.

"Your birthday," angrily retorted the officer, "why, you told me the very same thing a week ago, and, if it were your birthday, is that an excuse for drinking until you become a beast?"

"No, Sir," said the culprit, "it's no excuse, it's only a custom."

"How many more birthdays shall you have this year, you good-for-nothing drunkard?"

"It is very hard to say, Sir," stammered the sot in reply. "I make it a point to keep those of all my family, and I have a great many brothers and sisters, besides uncles, aunts, cousins, and distant relations."

The Saucy Jack. By a Blue Jacket. (London, 1840.
Richard Bentley.)

--------●◎●--------

To this harangue Classic, who had by this time got a seat and taken up a book, very coolly replied, "Come, old Squaretoes, don't give yourself airs, you only make yourself more ridiculous!"

"Airs, indeed," retorted the indignant Weazel, "here comes a pig to be shaved! I chuse to be ridiculous, sir; damn me, I will! and what's that to you? The first word you gives me in the way of *names* or *insult*, you shall see who you have to deal with—shiver my timbers!" "Bah!" cried Classic, "you're not fit to carry guts to a bear!" At this retort, the little master danced about in an ecstacy of rage. "You hear, gentlemen, I call you to witness, Mr. Sly—Mr. Belair, I call you to witness: gentlemen—you hear what he says, that I, the master of this here frigate and a commissioned officer ('No, no, you're only warrant, old boy,' cried Belair, from his cabin), that I am not fit to carry guts to a bear! to a bear! guts! mind that—guts! mark that! I'll soon see by G—d whether I'm fit to carry guts to a bear or not, da—n—tion; we shall see that in a shake! We shall see that! a bear, eh!" So saying, the enraged master darted into his cabin, and unlocking his desk got out pens, ink, and paper, and quickly indited the following letter, which, flying up the ladder, he shortly after delivered to the captain with his own hand:

Sir,—Being peasable behaved, and not interrupting no one, but in the line of my dooty, Mr. Classic is always after me, which is more than a man can barè; and now about the tie rimers, which he knows nothing about, and says you and I don't!—which I'll prove. I herebye require you, sir, to be pleased to write for a Corte marshall on the thurd Leeftenant, Mr. Classic, for having on this 20th of Febuary, in the year of our lord one thousand ate hundred and ——, called me, the Master to Command, of the frigate *Appollo*, under your comand, before good and suffigient witnesses, which I can proave, that I, Timothy Weazel, Master of the Navy, *was not fit to carry Guts to a Bear*—against the artakles of war, which do's not allow of no jibing, or calling names, to provoke the disiplin, under the king's pennant.

I am, sir,

with the greatest respect,
your obedient humble servant to comand
TIMOTHY WEAZEL
Master in the Navy."

"Given this day in my cabin
(before quarters) 6 p.m.
cloudy wr."

*   *   *   *   *   *

"Gentlemen," said the captain, "I am sorry for this disagreement. I am sure the slightest apology will satisfy Mr. Weazel, who complains of your having used certain *hard words* to him—and I am hardly mistaken, Mr. Classic, when I think you will make no difficulty in doing him justice, where his feelings may have been inadvertently hurt." "Just so, sir," cried Weazel, "let him unsay it, it's all I axes! let him unsay it."

"I am indeed, sir, very sorry to have said that Mr. Weazel was '*not fit to carry guts to a bear,*' I believe that was my expression, was it not?" "Yes, yes, sir! that was it—that was it; pretty thing, indeed," cried Weazel. "Well, sir," returned Classic, "I can only say, since it is so much insisted on, that I here now, before the captain, unsay it, and acknowledge that I am very sorry for having supposed Mr. Timothy Weazel *unfit to* '*carry guts to a bear,*' and I humbly retract the rash expression, and shall be at all times happy to bear witness, that he *is fit.*"

The Navy at Home. (London, 1831. William Marsh.)

—•—

When Admiral Pakenham, one of our renowned naval officers, landed at Portsmouth, a friend asked him how he had left the crew of his ship? "Oh," said he, "I have left them all, to a man, the merriest fellows in the world." "How so?" asked his friend. "Why," replied the Admiral,

"I flogged seventeen of them and they are happy it is over; and all the rest are happy because they have escaped."

The Log Book, or Nautical Miscellany. (London, 1826-7.
J. and W. Robins.)

———◆———

An Irishman, who served on board a man-of-war in the capacity of a waister, was selected by one of the officers to haul in a towline of considerable length, that was towing over the tafferail. After rowsing-in forty or fifty fathoms, which had put his patience severely to the proof, as well as every muscle of his arms, he muttered to himself, "By my soul, it's as long as to-day and to-morrow!" "It's a good week's work for any five in the ship! Bad luck to the arm or leg it'll leave me at last! What! more of it yet! Och, murder! the sa's mighty deep, to be sure!" When, after continuing in a similar strain, and conceiving there was little probability of the completion of his labour, he stopped suddenly short, and addressing the officer of the watch, exclaimed, "Bad manners to me, sir, if I don't think somebody's *cut off the other end of it!*"

The Log Book, or Nautical Miscellany. (London, 1826-7.
J. and W. Robins.)

———◆———

SAILORS ON HORSEBACK

When they were fairly out on the road, "Well, I'm blessed, but this here's a rum go, anyhow," said Joe Blatherwick to his messmate, as they rode alongside of each other, each ambitious to display his horsemanship to the best advantage, in the presence of the outriders in the dicky of the carriage. "We've got a couple of clean-going craft, that's for certain; but somehow or other I don't understand the heaving and setting to the swell, as I've seed some of the genelmen practice; and as for these here gilguys and head-braces, according to my notion o' things, they ar'nt rove as they should be."

"Why, shipmate, they do run somut crojack-brace fashion and that's the truth on it," replied Hardover, trying to lift in his saddle to the motion of the animal's trot; but this here pulling a-head, where a man has to rise from his thwart every time he stretches out, jist puts me in mind o' the Porteegeeze bargemen, when they keeps stroke by the whistle. And then to have the tiller-ropes leading forud instead of aft is enough to puzzle a man as has been used to steer with a wheel. Yet arter all, messmate, we ought to be grateful for being where we are, for we've overhauled a lesson in life within these few days as ought to be entered in the log-book of memory till we heaves short to trip the anchor for the last time. It should make us think upon our latter eend, Joe."

"Latten eend, Jem!" uttered the boatswain's mate, who took the matter literally; "why so it does, messmate—so it does—for mine's getting most confoundedly chafed with this here leather consarn as is under me, and I'm blessed if it ull let me forget it."

Jem Bunt: A tale of the Land and the Ocean. By the Old Sailor.
(London, c.1845. Willoughby and Co.)

APPENDIX A.

BIBLIOGRAPHICAL NOTE

Naval fiction relating to the period 1793–1815 begins to appear in 1804. With the exception of The Post Captain, *however, by John Davis, which ran into eight editions between 1805 and 1846, these early novels are of little value. There was a widespread interest in the Navy during the years 1805–1815 and the verses of Charles Dibdin, which had reached a large public in 1796–1805, were still popular. But there was little fiction written, mainly perhaps because the future authors were still on active service. After 1815 there was evidently a post-war reaction causing publishers to reject MSS. of naval character.* The Adventures of a Post Captain *appeared, in verse, in 1820, but public interest was then, probably, at its lowest. Nor did it revive for another five years. It was presumably the Burmese War (1824–5) and the Battle of Navarino (1827) which restored the Navy to popular favour. For in 1826, with the appearance of* The Log Book or Nautical Miscellany, Greenwich Hospital, *and* The Naval Sketch Book, *a flood of naval fiction came on the market. Captain W. N. Glascock had set the fashion and Captain Frederick Marryat followed with* Frank Mildmay *in 1829, the year in which* Tom Cringle's Log *began to appear in* Blackwood's. The King's Own *came out in the following year, Neale's* Cavendish *in 1831, and Chamier's* Life of a Sailor *in 1832. The output of such books reached a peak in 1836–41 and then slowly declined until about 1856. By that date many of the veterans were dead and the Crimean War had come to interrupt the reminiscences of those who remained.*

The merits of these authors, or most of them, are discussed in Commander C. N. Robinson's book, The British Tar in Fact and Fiction *(published in 1909), to chapters XV to XVII of which the reader is accordingly referred. Published, for the most part, by Henry Colburn or Richard Bentley, many of these novels were originally anonymous. About the authorship of some there has been, as a result, some confusion. Rattlin the Reefer, for example, was for long attributed to Captain Frederick*

Marryat, and The Post Captain *as wrongly ascribed to Dr. J. J. Moore, the author of* The British Mariner's Vocabulary *(published in 1801). The authorship of other novels remain obscure; and of some of the authors named little or nothing else is known.*

In assessing the value of these works it is important to know what experience the authors had and at what period they gained it. John Davis was at sea from 1787 to about 1798 and in the Navy from 1793 to 1797. He was not an officer. Glascock was born about 1784 and entered the Navy in 1800, rising to Captain before he retired. Frederick Marryat was born in 1792 and served from 1806 until his retirement as a Captain in 1830. Edward Howard (d. 1841) was Marryat's shipmate and went to sea about the same time, afterwards collaborating with him in the Metropolitan Magazine. M. H. Barker, who wrote under the pseudonym of "The Old Sailor," was born in 1792 and saw service both with the East India Company and in the Navy, but was not commissioned. Frederick Chamier was born in 1796, joined the Navy about 1810 and served until his retirement as Captain in 1833. Michael Scott, born in 1789, travelled to Jamaica and elsewhere but was not a sailor. W. J. Neale was born in 1812 and served from 1824 until about 1830, without obtaining a commission. Captain Basil Hall was not exactly a novelist. He went to sea in 1802 and his literary work, which is valuable, dates from between 1831 and 1856. James Hannay's service was later than the others, covering the years 1840 to 1845.

For ease of reference a table is subjoined, showing both the works quoted and other contemporary works, in their chronological order. The list, incomplete as it must be, will give, nevertheless, a fair idea of the literature from which the extracts quoted have been drawn.

APPENDIX B.

NOTE ON THE ILLUSTRATIONS

1. PORTSMOUTH POINT. *Rowlandson's viewpoint was in what is now called Broad Street, looking north along the moorings opposite the Gun Wharf and the Dockyard. He was facing up the harbour with his back to Spithead. Old Portsmouth has suffered heavily in the recent war and, of the buildings Rowlandson saw, few have survived undamaged. The Star and Garter Inn, visible on the right of the picture, is still there, but sadly altered by the combined result of Victorian improvement and enemy action. See Plate 9.*

2. PLATE 1. *Rowlandson did a series of water-colours showing naval uniform as worn by all ranks towards the close of the wars after epaulets had come to be worn. Others of the series may be seen at the National Maritime Museum.*

3. PLATES 2, 3, and 6. *To ascertain the internal arrangement of the old men-of-war is not easy. The Sheer Draughts, Profile Draughts and Plans which the builders prepared, and of which many survive, are useful up to a point. But with the allocation of the deck space the builder was not concerned. And the seamen, whom it did concern, were not always telling each other what everyone knew. A further difficulty is to decide the extent to which internal arrangement varied at the whim of individual captains. The cabins were lightly partitioned off in wood and canvas and most of them could be (and were) swept away when the ship cleared for action. The illustrations give no more than a rough idea where people berthed, accurate enough to enable the reader to understand references in the text. In Plate 1 the after guns are shown more or less in position near their posts. In peace time they were sometimes run forward or even struck below. Some captains (see p.73) kept their Great Cabins undivided.*

4. PLATE 5. *The model shown has part of the deck planking removed so as to show the structure and inward works.*

5. PLATES 7, 11, 13, AND 14. *These diagrams are intended merely to enable readers to follow the meaning of the text. They are a greatly simplified version of the actual sail and rigging plan of the period.*

6. PLATE 8. *The frigate "Foudroyant" now lying in Portsmouth Harbour alongside the "Implacable" is the only frigate still afloat in English waters, although there are two frigates surviving in the U.S.A. She dates from a later period than that of the French Wars but is not essentially different from the earlier ships.*

7. PLATE 9. *Of the buildings shown in this sketch, probably that on the extreme right is the only one now appearing roughly as Rowlandson saw it. Several on the opposite side of Broad Street are similarly unaltered. But all the east side of Broad Street has suffered heavily and the "Star and Garter", with its immediate neighbours, stands more or less derelict.*

8. PLATE 12. *H.M. Ship "Implacable" is an actual survivor of the Nelson period, having been in action, on the French side, at Trafalgar. At present (1948) it is possible to see examples of the three-decked ship, the two-decked ship of the line, and the frigate, all in Portsmouth Harbour. It is a state of affairs too good, apparently, to last.*

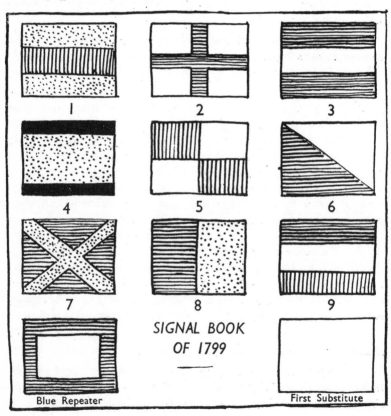

138

APPENDIX C.

GLOSSARY OF TECHNICAL WORDS USED

After-Guard: A ship's crew was divided into those who stood watch and the idlers, who did not. The former were divided in each watch into Forecastle-men, Topmen, After-Guard and Waisters. The After-Guard was composed of the slower, stupider seamen, together with landsmen. They worked the mizzen or spanker, the mainsail, and lower staysails.

Avast hauling: "Avast" means "enough" or "stop."

Belay, to: To secure a rope by a turn round a cleat or belaying-pin. Hence, to finish something.

Bend a sail, to: To bend a sail is to attach it to its yard or stay. A new sail is bent when one is worn out. The same term can be applied to clothes or headgear.

Best Bower: The bower anchors were the two most commonly used, being carried in the bows of the ship. They were of much the same size, the best bower being the one on the starboard side.

Boheaing-Hyson-Mundungo-built beggars: Bohea and Hyson are two sorts of tea, the carrying of which from China formed the East India Company's chief commercial activity. Mundungo is a corruption of a term used in Indian ship-building, more applicable to country-ships than to the Thames-built East Indiamen.

Booms: Booms were poles or light spars used to extend the foot of sails. They were kept amidships between the main and foremast and between or beneath the ship's boats.

Boxhaul: Box-hauling was a method of wearing or turning a ship when tacking and veering were alike impossible.

Braces: The ropes used to brace or pull the yards round according to the wind or course of the ship.

Brails: Ropes used for temporary trussing-up, as opposed to furling a sail, especially the mizzen sail and mizzen staysail.

Cable: A thick, three-stranded hempen rope, to which the anchor was made fast. The cables were made 120 fathoms in length, and a cable was thus commonly used as a unit of distance (i.e., 240 yards).

Carronade: A short piece of ordnance, mounted on quarter-deck and forecastle, firing a heavier projectile than a gun of the same weight would have fired, but effective only at a short range. Introduced in 1779, they gained steadily in popularity until 1812.

Cat-Heads: Two short timbers projecting over the ship's bows, one on either side of the forecastle, and used to suspend the anchors clear of the ship.

Caulking: Filling between the planks of a ship's side or deck with oakum, driven in with a chisel-shaped caulking-iron and coated or "payed" afterwards with hot pitch and rosin. The ship was thus made watertight.

Cockpit: A part of the orlop deck, at the after-end, used in ships of the line as the midshipmen's berth and, in action, as the surgeon's operating theatre. In frigates the midshipmen berthed in the steerage.

Collier: A collier was a vessel employed in the coal trade. She was usually a "Geordie" brig or barque, trading mainly between the Tyne and London River but also visiting other English ports, and even ports in the Netherlands and Baltic. The coal trade was reputed to be the best—that is, the hardest—school of seamanship.

Corianders: Evidently a slang term used for money. A coriander is actually a plant of the carrot family with a strong smell.

Crojack-Brace fashion: The Cross-Jack or Crojack was the lower yard on the mizzen mast. As the mizzen sail was fore and aft, no sail was bent to the crojack, which was used merely to extend the foot of the mizzen topsail. Crojack braces were led forward and crossed, unlike the fore and main braces which led aft.

Cutter: A small single-masted vessel, with fore-and-aft mainsail, foresail and jib, usually at this period rigged with a square topsail and top-gallant-sail. Cutters were used in the Revenue Service and in the Navy for carrying dispatches in home waters.

Day's Work: The observations and calculations by which a vessel's position was ascertained at least once a day, visibility permitting, and marked accordingly on the chart and entered in the log-book. Midshipmen did the process independently as part of their training, but it was not on their results that the Captain relied.

Driver or Spanker: A large sail which (c. 1794) was taking the place of the earlier fore-and-aft mizzen. Its boom extended far over the stern and the ensign staff disappeared to make room for it to swing.

Earings: Small ropes used to fasten the upper corners of a sail to the yard. One end was spliced to the cringle in the corner of the sail, the other passed half-a-dozen times round the yard and through the cringle.

Fishing an anchor: When the anchor was weighed and brought to the cat-head (i.e., "catted") it became necessary to draw up the flukes and stow the anchor. The hook, block, and tackle used for this purpose was called the fish, and the process termed "fishing the anchor."

Flying Jib: The jib was a triangular headsail, set between the jib-boom and the foremast. The flying-jib was a similar sail set outside the jib.

Forecastle: A short deck in the forepart of the ship, in much the same plane as the quarter-deck. It extended abaft the foremast, terminating with the galley chimney and ship's belfry. The word was also used of the space under the forecastle.

Gaff-Topsail: A fore-and-aft topsail set between the mizzen topmast and the spanker gaff in vessels (such as barques) which had no square mizzen topsail.

Gammoning of the bowsprit: The bowsprit had to take a considerable strain from the stays supporting the foremast, and was held down accordingly by seven or eight turns of a rope which passed through the stem or knee of the head, the several lengths being then frapped together.

Gangways: The narrow platforms connecting quarter-deck and forecastle in a deep-waisted ship, obviating the need to descend into the waist while passing from one to the other.

God-above-all: Presumably a name for a fancy piece of canvas—a "kite" — set above the skysails.

Gripes: A vessel's tendency to run up into the wind, which was, up to a point, a useful quality. But too much weather helm was again a fault.

Ground Tier: The lower part of the hold, the belly of the ship, where the provision and water casks were stowed.

Guard-Ship: Usually an obsolete man-of-war, permanently moored in harbour and used for the reception and temporary accommodation of seamen.

141

Guineaman: A Guineaman was a Slaver. On the Middle Passage the mortality among the slaves was sometimes high, and sharks were said to follow a Slaver for the sake of the bodies thrown overboard.

Guy: The name applied to a tackle primarily used to prevent a boom from gybing, but also used for other purposes.

Handsomely: Steadily—not too violently.

Half-deck: The space covered by the quarter-deck, comprising—in a frigate—the captain's cabin and, more particularly, the space just forward of it and under the break of the quarter-deck.

Hawser: A small three- or four-stranded cable laid "against the sun." It was used for warping and towing, etc.

Head or Heads: The forepart of a ship, comprising the timbers which projected beyond the stem and below the bowsprit, supporting the figure-head. It was used as the seamen's latrine, and the phrase "to go to the heads" has still its original meaning.

Head, captain of the: An old seaman placed in charge of the head.

Head, too much by the: The trim of a ship depended on the stowage of her hold. It was important that she should draw the proper depth of water fore and aft, to make the most of her sailing qualities. Most ships were stowed so as to bring the greater weight slightly towards the stern. When this rule was not observed, the ship was "too much by the head." But the head of a ship had a special purpose (see above) and the reference on page 109 has a double meaning.

Headrails: The timbers which formed the forward extension below the bowsprit supporting the figure-head and comprising the "head" of the ship. Thus, metaphorically, the head of a person.

Horse-Fly or Horse: A footrope extended parallel to, and about two to three feet below, a yard, supported at intervals by ropes called stirrups, and used for a footing by the men engaged in loosing, reefing, or furling the sail.

Jib-boom: A continuation of the bowsprit, to which it formed a kind of topmast and to which it was attached by boom-irons.

Jib-of-Jibs: The jib was a triangular headsail set between the jib-boom and the foremast. The flying-jib was set outside it and the jib-o'-jibs outside that again.

Jury-mast: A temporary and usually miniature mast, rigged to replace one lost in action or in a gale.

King's Bencher: A variant of Sea-Lawyer; an argumentative seaman "agin the government" of the ship and the Service.

Lanyard: A short piece of rope or line used, for example, to raise the gun-port lids, and to tauten (by means of dead-eyes) the shrouds which gave lateral support to the masts. Guns fitted with flint-locks were fired by means of a lanyard.

Lee-wheel: When there was more than one man at the wheel, the seaman on the lee side was the assistant.

Liner: As used at this period, the word liner is a slang term for a ship of the line.

Loblolly Boys: Boys or men detailed to assist the surgeon as sick-bay attendants.

Lobster-backs: The sailors' name for the red-coated marines.

Locks, Cannon: Firing guns with lighted match applied to the touch-hole with a linstock had serious disadvantages: one being the risk of fire. To ignite the priming powder with a flint-lock, as used in a musket, was an obvious improvement. First tried under Lord Anson, and later improved by Sir Charles Douglas (c. 1780), the detachable gun-lock was, by 1800, in fairly general use. The trigger was actuated by a lanyard, but the older method was still taught, in case the lock should misfire.

Manton Pistols: Mr. Joe Manton was a famous London gunsmith, maker both of sporting weapons and pistols.

Master-at-arms: The personage responsible, with the ship's corporals, for discipline and for detecting and arresting gamblers, drunkards, and other offenders against the King's Regulations.

Match: Cord soaked in resin and sulphur, lighted by flint and steel, and used, with a linstock, for firing the guns. See under "Locks."

Messenger (or Voyal): A rope, a part of which was wound round the capstan and another part fastened to the cable by short lengths of rope called "nippers." As the cable was too cumbersome to pass round the capstan, the capstan's energy was transmitted to it in this way.

Mizzen-staysail: A sail set on the mizzen stay and thus over the fore-part of the quarter-deck.

Moonraker: A light sail rigged above a sky sail.

Mugen: Perhaps a corruption of "Mudian"—i.e., Bermudan craft noted for their speed.

Nettings, hammock: The waist of the ship was protected on either side not by bulwarks such as flanked the quarter-deck but by iron standards supporting two net or canvas screens. Between these the hammocks were stowed, forming a bullet-proof breastwork protecting the sail-trimmers and small-arms men in action.

Orlop Deck: An incomplete deck, the lowest in the ship, used for cables, store-rooms and cockpit.

Points, Reef: Flat pieces of cordage fastened to the sails by eyelet holes in the reef bands. In reefing, the sail was hauled up by the reef-tackles and folded by the men on the yard, the reef-points being then used to secure it.

Prize-Money: A captured merchantman and cargo, if duly condemned by the Prize Court, was sold for the benefit of the captors. The sum thus raised was divided in fixed proportions among the officers and men present at the capture, the Captain of the ship being the chief gainer but also the person liable to be sued for unjustifiable detention of a ship not condemned. Flag officers profited by a smaller share spread over the whole number of ships acting under their orders.

Quarter-deck: This, in a frigate, was the deck which covered the captain's cabin, extending nearly as far forward as the mainmast.

Quarter-Gallery: A covered balcony, built at the after-end of the cabin and steerage and used as the officers' latrine.

Quartermaster: A petty officer who was often stationed at the wheel and whose duties might include the stowage of hammocks in the nettings.

Reefing Sails: Sail area was reduced by hauling up the head of square-sails and securing a portion of them by the reef points (see under "Points"). The topsails, being the largest sails, were made so that four reefs could be taken in. The mizzen sail or spanker was reefed from the foot.

Ring-Tail: A small quadrilateral sail, extended on its own mast, and sometimes rigged at a ship's stern, with a boom projecting outboard somewhat as in a yawl.

Royals: The sails set on the top-gallant masts immediately above the top-gallant sails.

Rudder-chains: Chains attached to the after edge of the rudder, by which it could be worked in an emergency.

Salt Junk: Junk is old cable or cordage. Salt junk is preserved beef of a similar texture and age.

Scowbunking Lubber: A scow was a large flat-bottomed boat used as a lighter or ferry. A lubber was a landsman. It may safely be assumed that the term "scowbunking lubber" was not a compliment.

Sea-Lawyer: An argumentative sailor "agin the government" of the ship and the Navy.

Sheep-shank: A knot by which a rope, found to be too long for convenience, might be temporarily shortened.

Sheets: The ropes fastened to the lower corners of sails to hold them in position.

Shores or Stanchions: Upright timbers on the centre line of a ship's deck, installed like pillars to take the weight of the deck-beams above.

Skyscrapers: Small, light sails, occasionally set above the Royals when the wind was faint.

Slings: Yards in men-of-war were prevented from falling, especially in action, by chain slings in addition to the halyards and lifts.

Small Bower: The bower anchors were the two most commonly used, being carried in the bows of the ship. They were of much the same size, the small bower being the one on the larboard or port side.

Smoke, to board in the: When alongside an enemy ship, or in collision with one, an attempt might be made to board her and finish the action with pistol and cutlass. Such an attack was usually made under cover of the smoke from the last broadside.

Soundings, to be within: To be in water shallow enough for the depth to be ascertained with the deep-sea lead: hence, to know one's whereabouts.

Spritsail: A sail bent to a yard slung under the bowsprit, and provided with holes in the lower corners to empty it of water when the ship pitched.

Sprit-topsail: A sail bent to a yard slung under the jib-boom and thus above and outside the spritsail.

Stays, a ship in: A ship was in stays when going about from one tack to the other.

Steerage: In a frigate the steerage was the part of the upper or gun-deck which was covered by the half-deck and captain's cabin. It comprised the officers' cabins and gun-room and owed its name to the tiller and tiller-ropes which led forward along this deck from the rudder head.

Stopper-overall: A stopper was a short piece of rope knotted at one or both ends.

Studding Sails (or Stunsails or Steering Sails): Light sails set beyond the edges of the principal sails and extended there by the stunsail booms by which the yards were prolonged. They were used in crowding canvas or in light winds.

Symondite Vessels: Sir William Symonds became Surveyor of the Navy in 1832 and revolutionised naval architecture by structural alterations, which were hotly discussed at the time. Ships built to his design, with the characteristic elliptical stern, were called Symondites.

Tackle of a Gun: Blocks or pulleys hooked to the carriage of a gun and to ring-bolts in the ship's side, enabling the gun's crew to run the equipment out after re-loading.

Telegraph: As used ashore in England, the telegraph was a system of semaphore posts by means of which messages passed quickly between the naval bases and the Admiralty. Afloat, the word signified the code of numerary signals perfected by Captain Sir Home Popham in 1803.

Tie Rimers: In the passage quoted on page 124, this is a misnomer for Triremes, the ancient vessels about which the ship's officers had been in disagreement. About the exact nature of a trireme disagreement is still possible.

Tiller-ropes: The tiller was the lever by which the rudder was moved from side to side. The tiller was connected with the steering wheel by the tiller-ropes, led, via blocks, up to the quarter-deck. Tiller-ropes were usually made of rawhide, as being stronger than hemp.

Top: The platform built round each lower masthead, and resting upon the cross-trees. It was used to extend the topmast shrouds and it was from there that the topmen started in loosing, reefing, or furling sails above the lower yards. The top was reached by ascending the shrouds and the futtock shrouds. No seaman was supposed to use the lubber's hole, the aperture in the top to which the shrouds actually led.

Top, captain of the: The Topmen were the most active seamen who handled the sails from the lower yards upwards, racing each other, mast against mast. The captains of the maintop, foretop, and mizzen-top were the petty officers leading the three groups of topmen in each watch.

Top-gallant yards: These yards, pronounced t'gallant, were set on the top-gallant masts and hoisted from the topmast-head when the top-gallant sails were to be set.

146

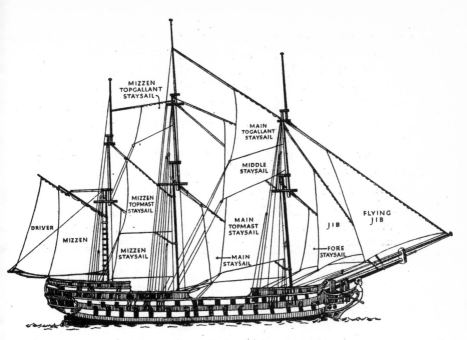

PLATE 13—Fore-and-aft sails of a 74-gun ship.

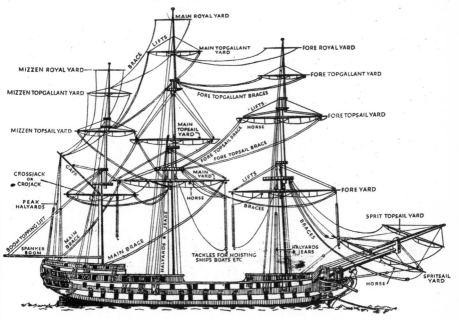

PLATE 14—Running rigging of a 74-gun ship.

Top-lights: Figuratively, eyes.

Topsail balliards or halyards: The tackles used in hoisting the topsail yards from their position when lowered (just above the tops) to the position just below the topmast-head in which the sail could be let fall.

'Tween-decks: There is a certain confusion about the names given to decks. In a two-decked ship there was the upper deck and the gun-deck. In a frigate there was an upper or main-deck which mounted the guns, and a lower deck on which most of the crew messed and slept. The latter was sometimes referred to as the 'tween decks.

Twicelaid: Old rope made up for use again.

Well: The part of a ship's hold, near the foot of the mainmast, from which water was drawn by the pumps. It was by sounding the well that the carpenter was able to report how much water had leaked into the ship.

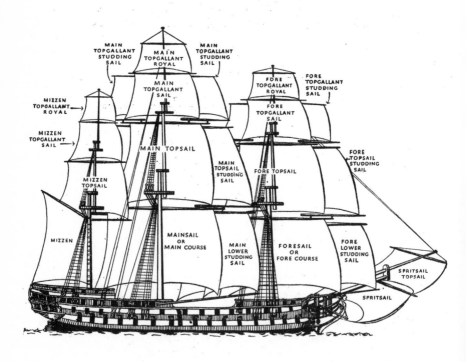

INDEX

The names of authors whose works are quoted in full are given under the heading "Authors," the names of their works under the heading "Books." The names of all vessels mentioned, real or imaginary, come under the heading "Ships."

Action, preparations for, 19.
Adams, William, loyalty shown by, 75.
Admiral, means of attaining the rank of, 21.
Admiralty, faultless appointments made by, 68.
Apprentices, exemption of, from impressment, 60.
Austen, Jane, naval interests of, 12.
—— character invented by, 21.
Authors whose works are quoted:
  Barker, M. H., 96–97, 99–100, 100, 100–102, 131–132.
  Chamier, Captain Frederick, 18, 50, 51–52, 57–58, 59, 60–61, 61–62, 63–65, 102–103, 107–108, 113–114, 124, 124–126.
  Davis, John, 22, 79–80, 84, 106.
  Dibdin, Charles, 13.
  Fletcher, Charles, 112–113.
  Glascock, Captain William Nugent, 25, 28–29, 37, 38, 65, 70–71, 83, 91, 106–107, 108–109, 111–112, 117–118, 122, 123, 126, 126–127, 127.
  Hall, Captain Basil, 56–57.
  Hannay, James, 23, 49, 53–54, 57, 98–99, 104.
  Howard, Hon. Edward George Greville, 32–33, 33–34, 35–36.
  Howell, John, 42–43, 78, 78–79, 80–83, 85–86, 86–90, 90–91.
  Marryat, Captain Frederick, 20, 26–27, 37, 40–41, 54–55, 65–66, 74–75.
  Neale, W. Johnson, 30–31, 37–38, 39–40, 48, 50–51, 56, 58–59, 94, 115–116, 122.
  Shakespeare, William, 14.
  Smith, Rev. G. C., 118–121.
Bacchus, a devotee of, 57.

Barker, M. H., sea experience of, 12.
Belair, Mr., Lieutenant, interruption by, 129.
Bell, ship's, the striking of the, 76.
Benbow School of Captains, 23.
Bennett, Tom, the comparative sobriety of, 95.
Berkeley, Master, the progress made by, 53.
Berth, Midshipmen's, the position of the, 16.
—— —— description of the, 58.
Bet of the Jetty, unpopularity of, 89.
Bibles, naval issue of, 116.
Bibles, hand, the use of, 79.
Birthday, as excuse for inebriety, 129.
Blackfriars Road, London, the Theatre in, 119.
Black List, undesirable use of the, 62.
Blackwall, East Indiamen at, 65.
Blatherwick, Joe, his latter end, 131.
Blue Peter, hoisting of the, 68, 79.
—— striking of the, 90.
Blue Posts Inn, Portsmouth, 98.
—— —— Coffee Room at the, 99, 100.
Blue Town, appearance of, at sunset, 90.
Boatswain, functions of a, 36.
—— anecdote of a, 122.
Books quoted:
  Ben Brace, Captain F. Chamier, 61–63, 63–65, 113–114.
  Biscuits and Grog, James Hannay, 23, 48–49, 53–54, 57, 98–99, 104.
  Boatswain's Mate, The, Rev. G. C. Smith, 118–119.
  Cavendish or the Patrician at Sea, J. W. Neale, 50–51, 94, 122.
  Dreadnought, The, Rev. G. C. Smith, 120–121.

149

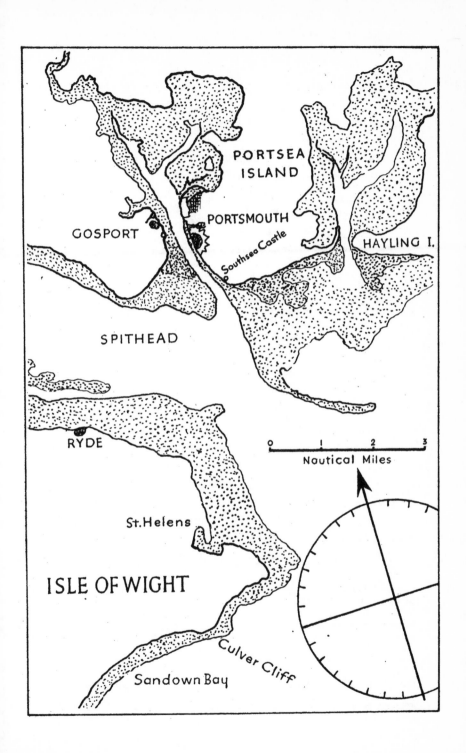

PORTSEA
ISLAND

PORTSMOUTH

GOSPORT

Southsea Castle

HAYLING I.

SPITHEAD

0   1   2   3
Nautical Miles

RYDE

St.Helens

ISLE OF WIGHT

Culver Cliff

Sandown Bay

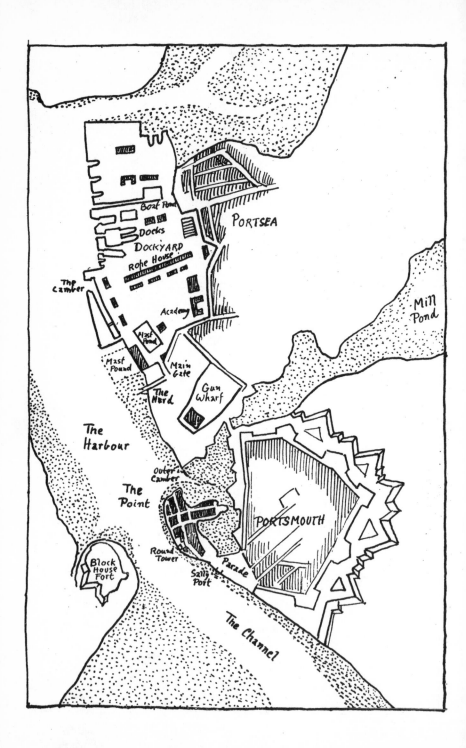